Texas
Bigfoot
In
My Backyard

The Second Year

Susan Sullivan

Texas Bigfoot In My Backyard

The Second Year

Authored by Susan Sullivan

Published by Purple Sage Publishing

Edited by Mark Angel

Copyright 2014 by Susan Sullivan

Table of Contents

Foreword

There will be times while reading this book you will ask yourself, "How can that be?" "There is no way a Sasquatch could be capable of that, but they are." Susan has seen it and told me about her daily interactions with the Sasquatches. For the short time I have known Susan Sullivan she has been honest and truthful and upfront with me about what is going on at the Bigfoot Ranch in Texas. Like most people, I wanted to find out as much as I could about Bigfoot. I had heard about Bigfoot many years ago as many of you have, but really didn't give it much credibility.

I thought maybe if it did exists it was only in the north western states like Washington and Oregon. I believed it had existed many years ago, but not today. Until I started watching the TV show Finding Bigfoot and they kept saying there were Sasquatches in every state. I couldn't believe it. In fact it wasn't till the start of the third season, that I really did start to believe. I started doing my own research, mostly online. Since I don't live close to an outdoor area nor do I have the time to venture out there. I knew I had to educate myself, so late in 2012 I started watching videos of people walking through the woods. Showing what a stick structure was and tree breaks walking along virtually with them. I watched a lot of videos. By the spring of 2013 I knew a little bit more about Bigfoot.

The Ohio Bigfoot Conference was coming up and what better way to learn than to go and listen to other researchers who knew. But there was only one problem, I wasn't able to get a ticket. Didn't really matter, I could still go and hang out with others and look around. As it turned out, my wife and I had a great time hearing a few stories and driving around Salt Fork State Park. At the time my beliefs about Bigfoot were much different than they are now. At that time I believed they were just flesh and blood creatures. I liked it better when I thought that. But the more research I did the more I was hearing about what a Bigfoot was and what they can do. At first I didn't want to believe it. I wanted to continue to believe they were apes running around the woods. But just like you are about to figure out by reading this book, I found out there is a lot more to Bigfoot then just wood knocking and howling. As I learned more I was able to put more thought into this subject. Now that's where Susan Sullivan comes in. I had seen her on Twitter mention she has a habituation site on her 100 acre ranch. She was offering to give out her email to anyone that wanted to see her pictures. Well I thought, if I want to learn she might just be the one to teach me. I emailed her and asked for any pictures and information she was willing to share. Susan was more than happy to share with anyone who wanted to see her pictures. After seeing the pictures I wanted more, I was hungry for as much as she was willing to share. I emailed Susan back and told her not to hold back, that I was very open minded and could handle anything. Susan started to open up slowly at first and maybe that was a good thing for me. For what she would tell me during the time I've known her would on many occasions just blow me away. I would many times have to take some time to soak it all in. As time went on Susan would tell me she read where someone such as herself asked for a rock from the Bigfoot people and got one. She thought, "Where's my rock?" And the very next day she got a huge rock. When Susan told me this a light went off. Why not try to ask for something else. Something I've heard about from someone else. By the spring of 2014 I had many experiences with Susan and her Bigfoot family. My outlook on Bigfoot has changed dramatically. I had attended the Ohio Bigfoot Conference for the second time, this time with tickets. My wife and I sat there and listened to the speakers. While listening to the speakers I realized they would only talk about one side of

Bigfoot. As I listened, I thought, if these people only knew, what I know now. Susan had confirmed everything I had learned before I met her and then some.
Mark

Thanks Mark for such kind words.

I consider Mark to be more than a Twitter follower, he is a friend. He introduced me to Mike Paterson's YouTube videos. He has also technically become my research assistant and editor. We have had a great time with new experiments during the Third Year. He makes suggestions based on all of his research, I do it and I actually get a response from the Bigfoot/Sasquatches. We are having a great time doing this. You will be amazed by some of the responses. For example, one day he asked for something specific from his house in Ohio, and I received the gift here in Texas! I plan to present many of these stories in the Short Stories Series. It will knock your socks off! Mark has helped me get over my fears. He is also the one person I know I can email any time of the day and say, "Oh My God!" "You are not going to believe what just happened!" I am so lucky to have met Mark and to have him join me on my journey on the path to understanding the truth behind Bigfoot/Sasquatch.

Susan Sullivan

Dedication

I dedicate this book to all the readers and reviewers who read the first book. Many of you emailed me after reading my books and shared your own personal experiences and drew me into your lives, and for that I am thankful, and I will never forget you. I would like to acknowledge those of you who emailed often, sometimes weekly and sometimes daily, I now consider you to be my lifelong friends and confidants. I dedicate this book to you, Mark, Molly, Patricia, Ladell, Lori, and Mike. I would especially like to thank you, the reader, for continuing on this journey with me and for offering me so much hope and encouragement. It is because of you I have chosen to write the Second Year book. This book like the first book is still *dedicated to my husband and children who still continue to live these experiences with me till this very day, and also to our visitors who still live somewhere out there and still come to visit our house on a weekly and sometimes daily basis.*

Prologue

The Second Year is the second book in the Texas Bigfoot In My Backyard Series. I had planned to write the First Year Book and be done with it. I was so shocked and humbled that people wanted to know more about me, my life and my experiences with the Sasquatches on the ranch. So I plan to continue to document my experiences to the best of my ability, and I plan to continue writing as long as people are interested in my story. The first book was very brief. I did that in order to appeal to the younger audience I was teaching. I know there were a lot of gaps and questions left unanswered. Heck, they were left unanswered because I didn't have the answers! This was all new to me too! The first book was all about my firsthand experiences as they were happening. It was totally fresh. I didn't wait twenty years to write the book. I didn't have the benefit of space and time that would give me the advantage of hindsight. I had just discovered and then had to learn to accept and process the reality that these creatures were part of our daily lives. This time, I plan to present a book that is much more thorough, and answer many of the questions that were emailed to me by curious readers.

So many of you wanted more details and explanations. For those of you who wanted to keep the conversation going, I offered you my email address in the previous books. This allowed us to get much deeper into the reality and much closer to the truth about Bigfoot/Sasquatch. I really appreciated the honest comments and thought provoking questions. I was excited to have the opportunity to communicate with such intelligent individuals about this phenomenal subject. I truly appreciate your willingness to come forward and discuss this topic with such insight and candor.

I started this book before the third year. I had so many people demanding the next book, so I quickly published a short story. I know a few people were disappointed. I can't believe people complained because I wrote too much about my every day family life. I guess those people missed the whole point by a mile. The whole point to all of this is not about my attempts to "Find Bigfoot", or to go "Squatchin" in the woods. I know that is what certain people are craving. I thought it was obvious and quite clear that I don't track them, hunt for them, or bother them. The whole point of my story and the whole series is that we happened to move to a ranch where there seems to be a relatively high occurrence of Bigfoot/Sasquatch activity and sightings. I have taken on the attitude that in order to honestly research, observe, analyze, document and come to a serious conclusion as to the true nature of these beings, I must not interject myself into their lives, but allow them to interject themselves into ours. I hold the belief that chasing and stalking them elicits a negative forced response, and gets no one closer to the truth. After all isn't that what we are all searching for in all of this? I would think so. I am not against researching these creatures in their natural habitat. I am against harassing and threatening these creatures and encroaching on their dens. I want to make it clear, I do not believe these are fuzzy, friendly, furry, teddy bears. I know what they are. I have firsthand experiences with these creatures. I am well aware of their physical strength, their weight and their mass. I am also aware of my physical inferiority and size compared to theirs. When we moved to the ranch we weren't even aware that these creatures existed. I did absolutely nothing that warranted the response we received when we first moved in. Knowing that I did not provoke these creatures, yet they set out on a campaign guaranteed to make most people turn tail and run, makes me well aware of their intentions and abilities. Therefore I must caution individuals who choose to create their own personal experiences involving Bigfoot/Sasquatch by going out into the wilderness and provoking them. Let me reiterate, this story involves my experiences of my interaction with these creatures at my home on a ranch in central Texas. I consider this environment to be safer, consistent, and much more predictable than traipsing into the nearby woods, which is something I refuse to do. I would never dare suggest to anyone nor would I condone such behavior.

So yes for those of you who are wondering, I am going to continue to discuss and present every day mundane descriptions of my boring family life here on the ranch. Because, guess what folks? That is where all of this is happening. This book is not about scary blood thirsty monsters lurking in the woods just waiting to attack and abduct innocent campers. It is not about my insane over the top maniacal responses to things unknown. This book is about Bigfoot/Sasquatch living somewhere out there beyond the ranch, beyond the trees and beyond the woods, and visiting our house still on a weekly and sometimes daily basis. Our attitude is very different than many others who have had Bigfoot/Sasquatch experiences and sightings. We are extremely cautious, and extremely respectful, and extremely aware that they are always out there just beyond our backyard, in the trees watching and waiting. For goodness sakes, people don't seem to realize I still have young children at home. We still fully do not know or understand these creatures, who they are, and what they are all about! I would be a damn fool to do something so heinous that would create such a response that would put my family in danger.

I realize that is where we are in this debate concerning the true nature of the beast. We have Bigfoot/Sasquatch hunting groups that have chosen to call them wood apes. We have groups that have chosen to call them fairies and aliens. The divide between the two is so vast. I believe the truth to all of this lies somewhere in the middle. I have chosen not to speculate on any of this until I have fully understood who these people are, and yes I am choosing to call them people. This is where I begin in the Second Year. This is what my attitude and experience would allow me to conclude during the second year on the ranch. Stay tuned however, because things changed drastically in the third year, changing my opinion, outlook and total understanding of who and what these creatures are. This experience was so terrifying that I had considered moving. This is why it has taken me so long to write the Second Year Book. What happened was so disturbing that I wanted out! I was so angry that I had refused to write another word.

It took me several months to take up writing again and to finish the Second Year Book. It was rather difficult since my perception of the whole situation had changed due to this new experience. I now had to go back in time and write the book as I saw things back then, over a year ago. I had to recall how I felt and what I truly thought then, without the benefit of foresight and the new experiences that redefined our perceptions of what we are truly dealing with today. This is much harder than it seems. I was being forced to suspend my opinion and judgment of current events. I became so bogged down in research, just trying to explain what had just happened to us. After this recent encounter at the beginning of the third year, I began to obsessively read all I could about the latest opinions of those few who can truly be called "Bigfoot/Sasquatch researchers", and whom shoulders many of us stand on today. For, without their knowledge, understanding, research and sacrifices from many years ago, we would be lost today. Many of these researchers have been in the field for well over forty years. To many of us they are better known as the "Knowers".

I soon began to delve back into the Philosophy of our thought processes and the psychology of our perceptions. I then researched what criteria is necessary to declare whether or not something is considered legal evidence, probative evidence, and scientific evidence. I did it all. I soon found myself spiraling into a deep dark black hole of vast amounts of information, and was totally lost. I then had to take a few steps back and realize that the reader does not care to know about the research, the proof, opinions, and scientific views and analysis. After all, those people don't have all the answers either. They are merely forming opinions, hypothesizing, and giving us their best guess, and then they change their opinions when they find a better answer. That is truly what science is. They are only trying to explain the inexplicable to us regular folks. Well, realistically "us regular folks" can really figure things out for ourselves. Some of us even went to college, and some of us have a little bit of common sense. I don't need someone else telling me what I did or didn't see, or did or didn't experience. I don't need someone else's opinion, especially someone who has never seen or had a Bigfoot/Sasquatch experience.

So, after all that research, I began to write the book. I had tied it all in and gave philosophical arguments and proof of the existence of Bigfoot/Sasquatch. I soon realized I sounded just like the "self-proclaimed expert/researcher" who descends from the heavens to proclaim whether or not some poor old country boy out hunting hogs actually saw a Bigfoot/Sasquatch or not. I made myself sick. I threw out the whole lot and started all over again. I also remembered how I felt when I bought and downloaded my first Bigfoot/Sasquatch book. I had no idea there were so many, until I had published my first book last year. I was so excited. I wanted to read all about their experiences, what they saw, what they heard, what they felt, and then how they reacted. That was all. I was so disappointed when the book I had spent my hard earned money on was written by some guy who had never had a Bigfoot/Sasquatch sighting. (Thermal doesn't count!) He had taken other people's experiences, opinions, research and stories and made them his own. I soon found myself rereading stories that have been told over and over again for the last forty years. I felt cheated and I felt lied to. I couldn't believe how many of these self-proclaimed experts have never had their own personal experiences, yet they are all too willing to give us their opinions and conclusions. Do you realize we are looking to these guys to tell us the truth?

I was prepared to start writing my book again. The only reason I was able to continue to write was due to my faithful friends who had read the first book. They constantly emailed me and encouraged me to continue. They insisted that I continue to write about my experiences and my truth, since that is what people were wanting to read. Besides, people are smart enough to form their own opinions. It is not our job to form that opinion for them. Our job is to simply provide our testimony, our experiences and what we believe our truth to be and let you decide. Since after all, that is what this is all about, my truth, my opinion, my observations, my experiences, my understanding and my conclusions, all based on what I know, what I have seen, what I have heard, and what I felt during the second year on the ranch. And that folks is all I have to offer, my story.

Chapter One

The Beginning Of The Second Year

The second year started out with a bang! I had just received confirmation during the Christmas Holidays that our property was known for having Bigfoot sightings and frightening encounters, not just recently, but twenty to thirty years before we ever moved to the ranch. Stunned by the new information, the kids and I reluctantly returned to the ranch after Christmas vacation, not knowing what lay ahead of us in the New Year. I began to prepare myself and my kids emotionally for the unexpected possibilities in dealing with this new phenomena that now defined our lives. There was no turning back now. We had decided to stay another year on the ranch. I don't think we would have ever been satisfied just up and leaving with so many question left unanswered. I mean, would you? Wouldn't you want to know who they were, and what they were, and where they came from? Well, that is exactly how we felt. We just had to know. We were now willing to accept our new reality and make the necessary adjustments to live in this new undefinable and unimaginable existence. I no longer sat outside in the dark on the patio. I did not plant flowers or vegetables, nor did I ever plan to. I never again ran outside and hollered at the moans, growls and howls in the pasture as I had done the year before. We did not go out onto the ranch and trim trees and have another fire until the end of the year. (The time between fires was twenty months.) We have also avoided the lake and pond, and have not taken the kayak and electric toy boats out onto the water. It all started to slowly sink in. They were right when they said, "Ignorance is Bliss." Total knowledge and total awareness sucks! It was as though we were living in a different state. I mean a different emotional and psychological state of awareness. We were always waiting for the next event, or disruption into our daily lives. We no longer reacted when we heard loud thumps or bumps up against the house. It just became our new normal. I must admit though, my heart would skip a beat, but we didn't run to the window to see what it could have been, we already knew. So this was how we prepared ourselves for the New Year. Our attitude towards our new life could be defined as a reluctant acceptance of what we could not control, but were desperately trying to understand. At this time I began to write my first book. I began to organize my timeline and my story and then I began the process of creating the book. This allowed me the chance to "get away" for a few minutes a day and throw myself into the writing process. It also allowed me to turn my fears around and face them head on. I began to share my experiences with my students at school for the first time. Up until this point I had not shared anything with anyone. I was pleasantly surprised when they did not react with fear and trepidation. Instead, they absolutely loved my stories. They couldn't wait for a daily update. These amazing kids did not view Bigfoot/Sasquatch as a monster either. They accepted the existence of Bigfoot/Sasquatch as just another phenomena that exists in our world today. I believe we have *Harry Potter* to thank for that. He taught our kids to believe in the mystical and magical realms that are just beyond regular folks' (*Muggles'*) understanding. It is just beyond the "Brick wall" in "*Dia-gon-alley*". I never realized how symbolic that was until we had our own experiences with the "supernatural". When discussing this phenomena, there is also a "Brick wall" that only certain people are allowed to go through. It requires one to have an open mind, an ability to see and hear the truth, and most importantly one must possess the ability to see beyond the lies that have been dictated to us since the beginning of time. How ironic is it that my students possessed all four abilities. They also saw nothing supernatural in the frightening yet beautifully natural experiences we were having on the ranch.

Students were so eager to read my story that one student insisted that I write an eBook. I am embarrassed to say, I had no idea what an eBook was and I had no idea what a Kindle was, but I was prepared for the challenge. It was hard. I had to research and read books on how to write an eBook. That alone took at least three months. This gave me very little time to research or read books on the subject of Bigfoot. All of my free time was spent trying to figure out how to write an eBook, and how to create it myself using my computer. Unfortunately, I was not computer savvy. Talk about old school, my computer was an old Dell. I used to laugh and imagine myself as one of those old time newspaper reporters who would only use their old trusty manual Smith Coronas. So I tapped away on my old Dell writing my story. Since I no longer had internet service at home on my home computer due to the constant disruption and disconnections in service, I had to travel over twenty miles north or over twenty five miles south to the nearest library in order to use the internet. I quickly learned how to write, format, edit, publish, and market an eBook. So, for anyone interested in writing and publishing your own book without internet service, it can be done. Use your local library. It is difficult, but it can be done.

The reason I am going into every detail is so that you can understand and imagine what an imposition all of this was. I want people to understand how much the Bigfoot/Sasquatches interfered with our regular daily lives. I had to go out of my way to create some semblance of normalcy for myself and my family. I also want people to realize that they have actually affected every aspect of our "normal" lives. This explanation I offer in response to several reviewers who could not understand why I spent so much time in my books talking so much about everyday mundane things in our everyday normal lives. That was the whole point. We in no way went out into the woods and interjected ourselves into their lives during preplanned scheduled occasions. They came to us. We had learned to just accept and live with these creatures who continuously reminded us of their presence. They were and still are very persistent. It wasn't as though they were trying to remain hidden. They made their presence known every chance they could, leaving subtle hints like balls in the yard and missing tools that would end up in odd places.

So, I continued to try and write the book with constant disruptions and without internet service. (Yes eventually I would get new service, but not till much later.) I also had to do my own editing, which I do not recommend. I thought I was going blind. I edited, and reedited, and reedited, and even then I made some mistakes. I am truly sorry for all the misspellings and weird sentence structures and grammar, of which I received two critical comments. I wanted to come across just as I had felt during my experiences, and how I actually sounded when I was relaying my story. Many of you got it! Thanks! You Get Me! My head was literally spinning with all of these thoughts and emotions, and I was experiencing real anxiety. I was also rambling to myself in my thoughts, even as I was writing and recounting these experiences, and I think that came across.

There is a very good reason why I did my own editing. I did not want anyone else to see, read, or edit my story. I also knew I could not handle the criticism. I was rather fragile, and I did not want to be judged. I mean after all, I had just become aware of the fact that the most amazing, phenomenal undiscovered elusive creature was visiting our ranch, sometimes nightly. As a university educated individual, I was wondering why I had never heard, studied, or been made aware of this creature during my undergraduate or graduate studies. I studied primates and their behaviors throughout the entire fossil record from the beginning of the known fossil record till I graduated from college. I also studied primate behavior in my Anthropology, Psychology and Sociology classes. The majority of accepted behavioral and psychological theories, scientific methods, and scientific principles were all based on primate behaviors and experiments that were carried out using primates, to get to these conclusions. Why was there never any mention of this creature anywhere in my textbooks? They are supposedly teaching current indisputable facts. Right? After all, that is what my parents were hoping, since they were footing the bill for my education at Southern Methodist University in Dallas Texas, and then graduate school through Texas A&M. So where was all of this information?

I had seen the Patterson/Gimlin film before, but I had no opinion concerning its authenticity. In other words, I placed no value in the media's presentation, or interpretation of the footage. I had always reserved my opinion on the whole subject of Bigfoot/Sasquatch. It never even really crossed my mind until I had my own experiences. Now I was able to form my own opinion based on my own information. I had my own personal experiences and my own eye witness sightings along with the eye witness accounts and experiences of my husband and daughter. I was shocked that the media, our institutions of higher learning, our government and the "scientific" community were ignoring this topic altogether. All I had to do was watch television to get an idea that the mainstream media had taken the subject and turned it into a money making cash cow and the butt of all jokes. I also knew that one "no", or one negative comment would have broken me and I would have stopped writing the book. You know what I am talking about. After going through all of this alone as a family, wondering about my own sanity, continually worrying about our safety and the safety of my children, combined with the possibility of being judged, it was all more than one person could handle. After all, I still knew nothing about this creature's intent, capabilities, or behaviors, of course I was worried for my family. I knew I was sticking my neck out there. I also knew I was not the only one out there who was asking these same questions. Why does there seem to be an ongoing systematic institutional and governmental denial of the existence of Bigfoot/Sasquatch?

I have to be honest with you, I was actually afraid to write the book. I was afraid "someone" would eventually show up on my doorstep and take me away. And by someone, I mean "the men in black", or whoever is responsible for keeping the lid on this thing. To proclaim, "there is something really strange going on here", would be somewhat of an understatement. To say I was in shock when I realized Bigfoot/Sasquatch existed, was not because I had just witnessed the creature with my very own eyes, I was more shocked that our society and our government, the media, and the "scientific" community were all ignoring the possibility that this creature may exist, no, more like covering up the fact that this creature does exist. So, that my friends is the real reason I self-published my own books. I was afraid I would be censored.

During the writing process I had to take several breaks. I did not realize how emotionally exhausting and intellectually taxing this would be. See, you have to understand, we still lived on the ranch. We were still experiencing ongoing activity at night and during the days, although subtle, it was still a nuisance. There were days I couldn't wait to leave the ranch. I worked overtime at my job that first part of the second year just to escape the ranch. I was actually afraid of being left alone on the ranch. There were so many days I would sit at the computer and begin to write and I would hear wood knocking, or worse, something would jump on the roof. I did not know if it was a cougar, the Juvy Squatch, or the Big Guy. I could not deal with that at the same time I was trying to collect my thoughts, figure all this out, and write the book. There was no escape. It wasn't as if I could leave the woods and drive one hundred miles back to my safe quiet house, get into my warm cozy bed, get a good night's sleep and forget about my encounters as many researchers do. I was still here, every day, and every night. And it wasn't as if I could schedule these encounters and fit them neatly into my vacation time. This was my life. Not just mine, my husband's life, and my children's lives. My husband had to continue to go to work every day and put on a brave face as if nothing was happening. (Oh who are we kidding, that was easy for him to do!) My kids continued going to school, and didn't dare share what was going on until we were 100% sure of what we were dealing with, and even then, my kids kept the information to themselves, for fear of being bullied, ridiculed and misunderstood at school.

So, for the first six months of the second year I was detached from all of the activity on the ranch. I took the kids in the morning to the cattle guard at 6:15 a.m. to catch the school bus and left the ranch and didn't come back home to the ranch till after work at around 6:30 p.m. If I was asked to sub for the day, I would take the job, or I would work at the library, anything to get away from the ranch. What was really sad about all of this, is that I was keenly aware that they (the Squatches) were ready for the next step. Yes, contact, communication, and eventually interaction. I knew they were getting closer and much more comfortable with the boys and with us in general. I, for my own sanity, had to completely block them out in order to keep writing the book. We received a little help in the form of another unwanted and unlikely intrusion into our lives.

Chapter Two

Other Creatures On The Ranch

We began to realize that we had not had a good night's sleep in over a year. We slept better when we visited Dallas. The bright lights of the big city, the sounds of car alarms, fire trucks and police sirens didn't faze us. They were actually comforting and we slept better at our house in Dallas during our visits there to see Daphene at college. For the first year, all the noises kept us up at night. The loud bangs and the subtle movements outside kept us all on edge during the first year. It was as though we were always waiting for a pin to drop. The silent moments were deafening and just as disturbing. Things on the ranch however became progressively worse during February, March, and April of 2013.

As I mentioned before, the second year really started out with a bang. We basically did not sleep at all for the next three months. Our county and three other neighboring counties were having wild hog round ups. They were paying hunters to trap, shoot and kill feral hogs for prize money. There is no season or bag limit on hogs in Texas. In other words, it was open season on feral hogs in Texas, and around the ranch. That meant we heard gunshots ring out at all hours of the day and night for three whole months. I was not a happy rancher. I was so worried about our Sasquatches and I was also very angry for many reasons.

First, I was angry because I knew blood thirsty ravenous indiscriminant hunters were in our woods. I feared for my Squatches' safety. Hog hunting has become a huge business here in Texas. Heck I have even been tempted to round them up and sell them at the local meat processing facility, but it is too dangerous. Most hogs are trapped in cages, corrals set up with trap doors, or they are trapped with snares. These hogs can weigh anywhere between 200 to 350 pounds on average. The most productive method to bag the greatest numbers for a competition, is shooting hogs, and that requires a landowner to pay $550 an hour for a helicopter service who can easily locate the hogs for the hunters. Hogs have been reported to run in packs of fifty to one hundred. I read on a few local websites that hunters shooting from a utility pole stand in the woods can take out forty hogs in an hour, sniper style. Whatever method they chose, our woods were not only infested with feral hogs, but with wild hunters as well. It isn't that we don't need help eradicating the wild hog infestation, I just hate being right in the middle of it.

http://www.tpwd.state.tx.us/huntwild/wild/nuisance/feral hogs/

http://feralhogs.tamu.edu/about/

http://ww2.txhoghunting.com/app/news/24744/Business-is-hog-wild-for-Milam-County-trapper

You should see the destruction first hand. A colleague at my husband's job totaled her car and was seriously injured in a head on collision with a huge boar less than a mile from the ranch. I saw the remains of the huge 400 plus pound hog on the side of the road. I personally have seen an entire section of our driveway uprooted as if someone spent all night tilling up the driveway. When we first moved in I had wondered why the fence surrounding the main property had barbed wire woven through the chain linked fence. I soon realized it was to keep out the wild hogs. There is evidence surrounding the entire fence line of digging and rooting up from the wild hogs trying to get into the main property. I can't imagine anyone attempting to plant and grow crops here on the ranch. They would completely destroy it overnight.

The second reason I was angry about all the hunting was because I knew that the hogs were a food source for our Sasquatches and the hogs were systematically being annihilated by the thousands every day. It turns out, according to a local expert trapper, that our Central Texas hogs are healthier and fatter than the East Texas hogs due to their diet. We are located in the woods of Central Texas, but just a few miles away, miles and miles of corn fields and wheat fields begin. So the hogs apparently fatten themselves up on grain in the farmlands, and then high tail it back to the woods for cover, just in time for dinner with our Sasquatches. This explains why the Sasquatches we have encountered here on the ranch are so huge. I have heard of seven and eight foot tall Squatches commonly seen in the Piney Woods of East Texas and the woods of the Pacific Northwest, and wondered myself why ours were so huge. I had a very jealous Twitter follower from the Pacific Northwest who refused to believe that my Big Daddy was ten feet tall. Really? Are we comparing sizes now? She viscously commented on her inability to understand why they were visiting the ranch, since I didn't feed them candy bars and go chasing them through the woods like she did. She didn't seem convinced when I tried to explain they came because of my bubbly personality!! (Just Kidding!).

I have had a couple of people ask about the Sasquatches "diet", and how is it that I can be sure they are actually eating wild hog. Well, first of all I call upon my common sense. Second I remember what a ten year old boy told me at my son's end of the year baseball party. The boys were all gathered at a table and began to tell scary hunting stories. I noticed one little boy who had a look of horror on his face that told me he knew. He then carefully began to recount his story, not sure if the other boys would believe him. He began to describe his hunting trip with his uncle. He said soon they came upon an area in the woods that left them speechless and terrified to go back into the woods. They had been tracking a hog. It was a rather large hog of three hundred pounds. By the time they had tracked it far into the woods, they were shocked to find that something or someone had gotten to their hog before they did. There before them, ten feet up in a tree was the very same wild hog they had been tracking through the woods. It had been placed high up in a tree wedged between two strong branches unable to move. He and his uncle did not care to stick around and investigate the scene. They fled. Human instinct took over and they ran all the way back to the truck and left the woods that day never to return. I can't imagine how terrified they must have felt. Wondering, questioning, reasoning and trying to explain what kind of creature would have the strength to lift a three hundred pound wild hog and wedge him in a tree ten feet off the ground. I could tell this young boy was still searching for answers. So I gently leaned over and said, "I believe you". He was so relieved when my son began to share some of our experiences here on the ranch. It all finally made perfect sense to him. He was satisfied, and like every normal ten year old boy, turned around and took off to play ball, not giving it another thought.

In my humble opinion, I believe that the overabundance of feral hogs on the ranch, and throughout the entire United States has afforded the Sasquatches a readily available year round food source that is high in protein, and most likely has resulted in a population boom in the Sasquatch community. I also believe this is why there are more sightings and reports of Bigfoot all across the country. How do I know this? Well first it is just plain common sense. Second, it happened to us. As a civilization and a species, once we began to eat meat and protein, our brain size increased. We basically went from eating twigs to eating meat about 1 million years ago. Due to the higher protein, our brain size increased and we then began to develop as a species and became civilized and socialized, then we eventually began to populate the entire earth. Eating and foraging on plants didn't keep us full and satisfied, so we spent the majority of our time foraging. The higher protein diet gave us more calories, which meant we spent less time searching for a meal, and more time to work on our social skills. Studies have been cited by Harvard, UC Berkeley and many other anthropologist who have studied the relationship between protein and brain size, and have put forth this theory. (Aiello, Rodrigo, Milton). They also concluded that due to the changes in our diet, we became civilized and therefore socialized due to a change in our behaviors. Having an abundant year round source of food, and consequently not relying on seasonal sources such as plants, also changed our social behaviors because there was less competition for food. Less competition means we behaved better as a civilization.

http://news.harvard.edu/gazette/story/2008/04/eating-meat-led-to-smaller-stomachs-bigger-brains/

http://www.washingtonpost.com/national/health-science/sorry-vegans-eating-meat-and-cooking-food-is-how-humans-got-their-big-brains/2012/11/26/3d4d36de-326d-11e2-bb9b-288a310849ee_story.html

http://www.berkeley.edu/news/media/releases/99legacy/6-14-1999a.html

I also found a couple of articles on the web suggesting that higher levels of potassium and magnesium in our local crops, and vegetation would be another reason our Sasquatches are so healthy. It would also contribute to more evidence and an explanation as to why they have chosen to be here near the ranch. I looked up potassium and magnesium levels as well as yearly rainfall totals here on the ranch, which seems to be higher than average. It is all starting to make sense. It isn't me after all! It is the food.

http://www.sunstar-solutions.com/BFgeological.htm

I cite these articles in order to explain why I believe the Sasquatches do behave differently depending on their habitat and their diet. I have read and heard others online berating and belittling others because they dare to claim that not only are their experiences different, their Sasquatches are too. You have Psychologists, and Anthropologists vehemently self-proclaiming their expertise in the field by putting down others and their experiences. Their claim is they are the authority and if your experience does not match theirs, then somehow you either did not have a genuine experience or you are lying. It just makes sense to me that different parts of the country offer different food sources. Different topography and different climates play a huge role in determining the varieties and different amounts of food that will be available to the Sasquatches.

Obviously, if our Sasquatches have a readily

available, mineral rich food source such as feral hogs and potassium/magnesium rich crops, and there is little competition for this food source among the Bigfoots/Sasquatches, then there is little need for such aggression between them and towards humans that is likely brought on by competition of limited life sustaining resources. Here on the ranch, even if the hogs were hunted to extinction, the Sasquatches would still have an abundance of deer, not to mention the same fields and food sources that the hogs once had. In the first year upon moving to the ranch, we had spotted a rather large herd of approximately twenty deer, which is rare anywhere. There seems to be a unique balance going on here at the Bigfoot Ranch in Texas. Yup, bigger hogs, means bigger Squatches, fuller bellies also means friendlier Squatches. Therefore, our Sasquatches feel less threatened, and therefore there is less of a need to exhibit such aggressive behaviors as others have described in their encounters. This explains their curiosity towards us and their willingness to interact with us by coming closer to the house and attempting to make contact on their own. This also explains why they don't take the few food gifts I have left out for them. They aren't hungry. They did however take my dishes, which I have not forgotten!

The third reason I was angry was because I knew it was a calculated disruption in their lives, just as it was in ours. Those hunters did not care that we lived nearby and had a family. They did not care that it was two and three and four in the morning and we all had to go to work and school the next day. They did not care that they were shooting in the direction of our house. I could not even let my kids play outside in the yard for the entire spring of 2013. (I am guessing the Sasquatch parents had the same reaction and response that we did.) We were just waiting for a bullet to come flying through the windows and hurt one of my boys. Last year I took a gun training class for women, and I was informed that a bullet from a rifle could travel over a mile. So, even though the hunters were not physically on the ranch, we could hear them in the woods nearby. What was really scary was the day my husband went to town to pick up a gallon of milk for the kids. He stopped at the local convenience store just ten miles down the road, and there were truckloads of hunters filling their gas tanks, and their ice chests. He witnessed camouflaged covered men purchasing cases and cases of beer. Great combination!! Camouflage, Beer, and Ammunition! Anyone see the big picture? Oh My God! No wonder they don't want to have anything to do with us! If I felt this way, and I was living in this much fear, can you imagine how the Sasquatches felt? Here is another thought. Can you imagine what these hunters would have done and how they would have behaved if they would have known that we had a clan of Sasquatches living in the woods? I cringe just visualizing these same camouflaged, beer packing, ammo hauling, and gun toting fools hunting for a Bigfoot.

I did contemplate on whether or not to title this chapter, "Everything Is Bigger In Texas". I know how arrogant that sounds and I am sure that is why that twitter responder was so jealous and treated me so unkindly. I have often wondered why we as Texans have that attitude. All I can say for now, is that yes, our hogs are bigger and healthier, and I explained why, which consequently makes our Sasquatches bigger and healthier and better behaved as well. No arrogance there, just reality. Another fact is that we don't have long harsh cold winters to contend with either. We have hot sweaty, humid summers, with bouts of drought and bouts of monsoons. We have more land, which means more game, and more crops to feed any growing population. No arrogance, just good old fashioned common sense.

Susan Sullivan

Chapter Three

All is Quiet on the Bigfoot Ranch

After the hunt and roundups were over in late April, we noticed an eerie silence fall across the ranch. We did not spot another hog for an entire year. When we did begin to spot the family of hogs, the herd was much smaller and they did not graze out in the open pasture as they had done before. They cautiously walked in the shadows between the huge oak trees, moving from tree to tree. It was obvious that the spring round up not only changed our behavior, but theirs as well. There was a noticeable shift. I was really sad and worried even though I was grateful for the peace and quiet at night. I kept wondering what could have happened to our Sasquatches. We would sleep with the windows open on cool nights so I could listen to all the sounds. I needed a sign that the Bigfoot/Sasquatches we have come to know were okay, especially the young ones. I needed to know that they were still there. Now that I know they are out there somewhere, I can never turn my back on them. I can never stop thinking about them. What was really strange was that during the first year I could not sleep because of all the activity, dogs barking, howls at night, and things being thrown at the house. Now I could not sleep because I could not hear anything at all. These were the moments when the silence was truly deafening. I desperately wanted to hear something so that I could sleep in peace knowing that they were okay. They have no idea what they have done to me. My soul was aching, and I feared I would never see or hear from them again. I was worried that the hunters had either scared them off or killed off their food source, or worse. (I would get my much needed confirmation two months later on a cool night in June. Until then my mind had time to search for all the answers that continued to nag at me.)

Eventually I became hypersensitive. I began to wonder if my hypersensitivity was beyond normal perception. I could actually hear the cattle lurking around in the pasture. I even heard the rattle of a rather large rattle snake under the juniper tree about thirty or forty feet from my bedroom window. How did I know it was large? I could tell by the rattle. It was obvious there were multiple beads, which increase based on the age and size of the rattle snake. I heard it three nights in a row. On the fourth day my husband went looking for it. He knew I wouldn't sleep until it was taken care of, I was afraid the boys or the animals would get bit. Yup, that is how sensitive I became.

After the hunters left I noticed there was an obvious imbalance on the ranch. More specifically, there was an obvious imbalance between the species. If the Sasquatches/Bigfoots were still lurking around the ranch, we didn't notice anymore. They became more cautious, quieter, and almost INVISIBLE. The coyotes however were louder and more brazen. They continued to come around every other week and especially during the full moon and this time in larger packs. This time they were coming closer to the house and there seemed to be more of them.

One day coming home from school the kids and I

came down the driveway and saw a beautiful female coyote with three pups. We were so close we could see their blue eyes. We could not believe that a mama coyote would have the pups so close to the house, just fifty feet from the second cattle guard, and only fifteen feet from the water main shut off valve under the huge oak tree. That was just way too close for comfort, and way too close to my front yard. She must have delivered them during the hog round up and she also knew that being closer to our house was much safer than being deep in the woods. Amazing how we were all thinking and behaving the same.

I started to wonder if we were dealing with coyotes after all. Now remember I had said before in the first book, that we had lived in New Mexico. Whenever I saw a coyote in New Mexico, it was always alone. I felt so sorry for the coyotes in New Mexico. They looked so skinny, scrawny, and mangy compared to these big guys. The first time I saw coyotes on the ranch I was shocked. I even wondered the moment I saw them, if they were possibly a hybrid, a cross between coyote and wolf.

I had a friend, Misty, in Taos, New Mexico who raised wolves, so I was familiar with their size, the color of their coats, and their demeanor. I also volunteered once at the dog shelter in Taos. My job was walking a gorgeous white wolf named Baby. We went for a walk among the fragrant sage brush just on the outskirts of Taos. To say that was a profound experience would be an understatement. Can you imagine, walking among the sage brush with a huge white wolf on a leash, in Taos, New Mexico? He was so gentle and his name was befitting. He cried like a baby in the shelter. He howled and groaned, as I am sure he missed his family. I guess his owners could not take care of him anymore, so they gave him up to the shelter. I desperately wanted to adopt him but I couldn't since I lived in a small apartment with my two year old daughter Daphene. We were recovering from a divorce, which led us to Taos New Mexico. So, once again, I am quite familiar with the subject at hand, coyotes and wolves.

One day when we first moved to the ranch, I spotted three adult male coyotes. I was in total shock. They were huge. I tried scaring them off by yelling at them. That would have worked with the puny coyotes in New Mexico, but not for these Texas coyotes. They looked at me as if I was crazy. (Yes, I will let you take a minute to create that mental picture of me yelling at coyotes in the pasture. Hey I had already conquered yelling at a Bigfoot, coyotes were nothing to me.) At first they circled back to the pond twice then they took a stance and stared at me, no, more like glared at me. They even began to come closer. That was not what I was expecting. It was broad daylight and they were not afraid of me. Unbelievable! There was no way these were coyotes. (We avoid having guns in the house, but after my brother had heard of the rather large bold coyotes, he gave me a shot gun and a box of ammo. I also decided to take a women's gun safety class. Never once did I consider this as a need to protect myself against the Sasquatches. Funny thing is, that once I mentioned my fear of the coyotes and began packing, I never saw another coyote during broad daylight.)

Well, since there was no sign of any Bigfoot/Sasquatches on the ranch during that time, I began to research Coyotes. An absence in Bigfoot activity did not necessarily mean a total absence of activity. As an observer intent on documenting everything, I became very aware of the subtle changes on the ranch, and it was my job to figure out the cause and come up with a plausible explanation, and

I began to do just that. A good researcher should research all aspects of their subjects, evidence, and lack of evidence, their environment when they are present and when they are absent in order to make honest comparisons. That is another benefit of a habituation site. The obvious consistency and the ability to make honest comparisons offers much more valid conclusions. Something you can't do running around the woods.

I found out through my research, that coyotes are solitary animals. They are much smaller than wolves. Those two significant details immediately led me to believe that I was not dealing with coyotes. Ok, now tell that to the local Texas Wildlife biologist/expert. Once again, can we all sing in unison? "There are no wolves in Texas!" Here is another favorite of mine from years gone by, "wolves and coyotes are different species therefore they cannot interbreed." These are long held scientific theories. I won't call them truths, since they have been disproven over and over again. We have been taught by the established scientific community that different species could not possibly crossbreed, and if by chance they crossbreed, they are sterile. So, which one was correct? They couldn't all be correct? I have very large coyotes on the ranch that roam in packs of ten to twenty, and they are obviously breeding. I say they roam in packs of ten to twenty based on the howls we hear at night. They howl in unison and consecutively, and I have counted over twelve distinct howls and up to twenty. (Just last night I heard the wolf/coyote pack, and this time I heard the puppies howl with the pack.) It is obvious to me it is a large pack. They can't be wolves according to the local Texas Wildlife experts/scientists, and they can't be hybrids, and based on their behaviors and characteristics, they can't be coyotes. Could it be that we may need to possibly redefine some of these categories and their characteristics. Were these long held "scientific" theories also documented out in the wild by randomly visiting researchers who caught a glimpse of an animal and consequently put these "theories" in writing therefore making them the golden rule of science? I'm just thinking out loud. Makes you wonder though. Who made up all these rules?

Here I am again, in the same spot I was in a year ago, thumbing my nose at the scientific community. No, I am not sitting here on pins and needles, chewing my nails waiting for some pencil pusher to make scientific declarations about the existence or nonexistence of yet again another creature that just so happens to be roaming the Bigfoot Ranch in Texas. And, by the way, creatures I have seen with my very own eyes and also within fifteen feet. Why do I bring this up? Well we are talking about long held scientific beliefs that we hold as truths. They are not truths, they are theories, which have been disproven and replaced with newer information about a developing species. That is all science is, hypotheses and theories. I also bring this up for the "few' people who are going to comment and say that I am off the topic and spinning off into random subjects. I will try and piece this together for you. "Scientist don't have all the answers!"

Check out these tracks!

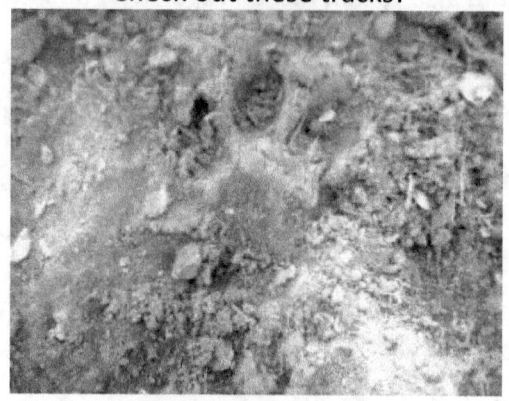

Figure 1 Cougar Tracks

Figure 2 Cougar Tracks

[FYI, here is evidence of another creature we have been told (by the regional wildlife expert) doesn't exist anywhere in Texas either. I found these cougar tracks right next to my sitting room window. The flower bed had been disturbed so the cougar had apparently been after a rabbit or a mole burrowing under the hedges. We have seen other cougar tracks on the opposite side of the house. This rather large cougar apparently makes its nightly rounds circling the house at night, brushing up against the four corners of the house, leaving a noticeable worn path. The property manager noticed the worn path, which I have tried to reseed twice, and commented on the dogs making the path. I said, no there is a much larger creature who paces nightly on that path. Had it not been for the rain showers the night before we would not have found these perfect tracks. I have not had an eyewitness sighting of the cougar, but I have seen the tracks, and heard the gut wrenching blood curdling screams that sounded like a woman is being raped in the woods. The sound is unmistakable and cannot be confused with the sounds, moans, and growls of a Sasquatch. The two species make very distinctly different sounds. I bought a game camera to capture images of the cougar, but I don't want to upset the Squatches. I have heard from more than one researcher that the Sasquatches do not appreciate game cameras.]

So, once again, during the quieter months I still heard the occasional coyote packs, which I now believe to be wolves or hybrids. (Or, are they super coyotes pumped up on all the good food sources around the ranch, just like the Squatches and the hogs? Hmmm...) I also suspected that our Sasquatches were still out there, even though we no longer heard their howls. I heard on a Bigfoot show that these coyote/wolf packs follow the Bigfoot much like dogs hang out with humans around the dinner table. They finish off whatever the Bigfoot doesn't eat. So, I soon began to realize that even though I could not hear the Bigfoots outside, I knew they were there as long as I heard the occasional howls of the wolf pack. That remained consistent throughout the rest of the year, until the howls of the pack also began to subside and they only came to the ranch once a month during the full moon. I am guessing that after the big hunt the Bigfoot/Sasquatches could not trust anyone, not even us. So where did they go?

At one point during the second year, due to the utter silence on the ranch, I began to believe that they had all moved away, or migrated due to the changing seasons and the unbearable Texas heat. This led me to research possible migration patterns of the Sasquatches. You are probably as shocked as I was to learn that yes, that research has been done. Thank God!! I was really afraid I would have to spend the next twenty years investigating, documenting, fact gathering, etc., etc... Guess what folks? It has already been done. How could there be so much documented scientific research on a creature that doesn't exist? Most of the data I collected was twenty to fifty years old, and obviously well established, documented field research. People just didn't sit around and say "Cool", after seeing the Patterson/Gimilin footage. People took it seriously, even before the footage, and they began to scientifically research the Bigfoot phenomena before I was ever born! There has been ongoing research and data collecting, and analysis for well over fifty years. And guess what? It really wasn't that hard to find. So I am totally baffled by all of these individuals who waste their time on the internet proclaiming the nonexistence of this creature, instead of actually researching the topic.

The information I did find concerning Sasquatches, states that they do not migrate, their behaviors change. (Wow, just like us!) For example, Sasquatches in the Colorado area near Gunnison tend to hide out in caves during the winter. They found stashes of food and a crudely made loaf of bread in a cave. In the researcher's opinion, these items were not left by humans. I was flabbergasted. There is more to this creature than we have been led to believe. I was beginning to see them in a different light. I began to see them as people. For one, they have been here a long time and have well established documented patterns of behavior. Second, there has been extensive scientific field research that has been ongoing for over fifty years, plenty of proof and evidence to establish and verify their existence. Third, I was thrilled that I didn't have to reinvent the wheel, and so I won't. There is plenty of scientific, field research and therefore, I will just stick to my own experiences. It does make me wonder and question, with so much scientific research, field research, and documented data that I was able to find, why people are still claiming there is no "scientific" evidence? (Oh I was also excited to hear about the loaf of bread! Someone is baking up there in them thar hills! Can you see it now folks! That will be my next book, A Bigfoot Cookbook! Wild Feral Hog Stew with a loaf of crusty Sasquatch Bread!)

http://www.bigfootencounters.com/biology/migration.htm

I thanked God and the Sasquatches on the ranch for a much needed break. It allowed me the time to write the first book, and it gave me the time I needed to research information so that I could get a real thorough understanding of what kind of creature/people we were dealing with on the ranch. In my opinion we were dealing with sentient individuals capable of reacting and responding to events such as the hog hunts. The change on the ranch had nothing to do with the seasons, the drought, or any supernatural occurrence. It was all due to human interaction and intrusion into nature. My research also allowed me to identify and understand the other creatures that visited the ranch. It all began to take shape. It all began to look like this perfect orchestrated dance of actions and reactions, activity and inactivity. I saw the connections and I became keenly aware of the intricate balance on the ranch. Just because we did not see them or hear their roars at night, did not mean they were no longer there. I instinctively knew they were still there lurking in the shadows just beyond my backyard. They were intentionally choosing to remain silent. I believe they were observing us, to see what our next move would be. Would we take up arms and join the rest of the hunters? Would we put up game cameras and start trapping hogs? I knew they were trying to sum us up, and in order to do so they must remain silent and continue to observe us. Till this day they have remained rather quiet. Since 2012 we have not heard the loud roars made within yards of the house that hit the side of the house with such force that I could feel the vibrations. All I hear now is them lurking around the house, an occasional loud hard bump against the house, and even once what sounded like a stampede right outside my bedroom window that was so loud and powerful that it caused the windows to rattle and vibrate. Once I heard a very small creature jump at the side of the house next to my bedroom window and climb the two stories to the roof. It sounded like a monkey, I am guessing it was the baby Sasquatch.

I often tell people, researchers and interested parties, there is no reason for them to come to the ranch. First of all I tell them the Sasquatches do not live here on the ranch. I had at one time believed they lived out in the woods. All this activity and subsequent inactivity got me to really question where they did go to hide out from the hunters. The woods were once their place of refuge and now they were not safe there anymore. So, I then began to research places to hide in the area, and once again I was given the perfect opportunity to continue my research.

Chapter Four
Where Could They Be Hiding?

I have learned in the past two years that there are no coincidences. I needed and prayed for the peace and quiet and I was blessed with exactly what I had asked for. The hunt had an effect on the whole family, dogs, cats and Squatches included. I began to wonder if they (Sasquatches) knew that and intentionally remained quiet, giving us the much needed rest. I continued to stay busy at work, and I was asked to teach a Geography class for the summer school program starting in May. My first reaction was that this must have been a coincidence, but the more experiences I have here on the ranch, I have come to realize there are no coincidences anymore.

So, I began my in depth research on the Geography, Topography, and Geology of the central Texas area, which would help me teach my summer school class. I also researched rainfall totals, lakes, rivers and streams in the area as well as volcanoes, caves, minerals etc., and the Native American history. This all allowed me to satisfy my insatiable desire to understand and gain more information as to why they have chosen to make their home here in Central Texas, and more specifically what makes them want to visit the ranch. I began to dig in deep and do some serious research. I wanted to figure out what made this a prime habitat for the Bigfoot/Sasquatches. Could they possibly be hiding in underground caves?

So all of this research served a dual purpose, I was going to teach my students everything I was learning about the area they call home. It also allowed me to research the various caves in the area, since we had planned to end the summer program by taking the students to Inner Space Caverns in Georgetown Texas as the Grand Finale. How perfect!

It is a well-known fact that the central Texas area has several "discovered" caves. These caves are located well within one hundred miles from the ranch, and along a fault line. The Inner Space Caverns in Georgetown Texas are about fifty five miles away. My summer Geography class took a field trip to the caverns in June of 2013, and my son Kirk's class took a field trip there during the school year as well. Everyone in the area knows about the caverns. There is no mystery about all the "discovered" caves in Central Texas area.

Inner Space was discovered in 1963 when the Texas Highway Department was constructing Interstate 35 south of Georgetown. As the highway was being constructed, a road crew was drilling core samples. When they reached a depth of 33.5 feet, they lost the drill bit as it fell into the cavern room known as the Discovery Room. They sent a crew member down a rope and dropped him into an enormous chamber. If you look up inside the cave, you can still see the original hole. The Highway Department Geologist James W. Samson had warned the drillers of possible caves in the area before drilling began. This cave is located within the Balcones Fault Zone and is characterized with a secondary cross fault that is easily visible and accessible to the public and is pointed out during the tour. It is believed that the cave had been closed off for 10,000 years. There were many sink formations where previous entrances had been blocked, or collapsed and caved in. Paleontologists found mammoth, camel, dire wolf, horse, and saber tooth tiger bones to name a few.

www.innerspacecavern.com

Another well-known cave in the area is Longhorn Caverns. These caves are west of Austin in the Hill Country, also less than one hundred miles away. These caverns are well known and had been used by Native Americans some 400 years ago. The Confederates also used the cave to manufacture and store gunpowder during the Civil War, and it was once a dance hall during prohibition. This cavern was formed by a river, as most caverns are.

www.longhorncaverns.com

There are the Natural Bridge Caverns near San Antonio. This cavern was discovered in 1960 by four college students, on a ranch near San Antonio. So, most known caverns are discovered by accident. This cave was also formed by an underground river. Cracks in the limestone allowed water to seep through and water dissolved the limestone therefore creating the cave. Water then drained to lower levels and created a deeper second level and possibly even deeper levels. Archaeologist conducted a dig and found artifacts to hunt with, to cook with and to make tools. It was obvious that Native Americans had also inhabited the entrances to these caves before they were "discovered" again.

www.naturalbridgecaverns.com

During the summer of 2013, I had heard on the news that there was a newly discovered cavern in Williamson County. It too was accidentally discovered by a highway construction crew. Once again during road construction a cave was discovered. The last I heard, the transportation department was discussing plans to fill the cave in with cement and cover it up. Yup, so typical. If that isn't ironic, yet symbolic of what is actually going on. Let's cover it up and fill it up with cement. Let's just ignore that it even exists. Then let's report to the world that there is "no evidence" of anything beneath our feet.

I had already known about all of these caverns, and have toured each one as well. I could not wait to explore the geography, topography and the geological makeup of the area. I knew this would help me explain how we could be living side by side a Bigfoot community and not know it. It turns out there is another cave closer to the ranch in the next county, maybe within twenty miles or less away from the ranch. I am dying to explore that one. It is privately owned and located on a private ranch. One key feature of all of these caverns is that they were all "discovered" by accident, which makes me believe there are many more we have not discovered, and that these discovered caves are only a fraction of a percent of all cave systems. Just because we haven't found them does not mean they don't exist.

Just a few nights before I added the finishing touches to this chapter, I decided to sit outside for the first time in two years and enjoy the crisp cool July evening, thanks to a cold front that came through. Rarely are summer evenings cool in July in Central Texas. We have had such a mild summer, and I finally had the courage to sit outside. It was all due to a friend of mine from Ohio, Mark. He had sent me an email with pictures of orbs, so I was curious and I wanted to see if we had any orbs floating around on the ranch. I was willing to try a few experiments that I will discuss later in the third year. I was shocked when I saw a bat fly by me. It was small and brown. I knew I had to research bats now, and I needed to find out exactly how far they are able to fly away from the cave each night. I found they could fly anywhere from half a mile to six miles. Some research suggested nine miles. There was such a difference in opinion, I wasn't sure if they were taking into account the return flight. Taking all of the data into account, and splitting the difference, we can estimate that these Mexican Brown Bats are cave dwellers and can fly up to six miles an evening. Which leads me to believe there is a cave within six miles of the ranch, even closer than the newly discovered cave in the next county. Hmm it is all making perfect sense now. All the other caves I had mentioned before are well over fifty miles away and some are much farther. Could this possibly mean there is a cave closer to the ranch?

During my research I learned that there is an aquifer and a fault line beneath the Edwards Plateau. It extends from the Austin area down to San Antonio. Water is the main force behind cave formations in this area, therefore water from the aquifer is a contributing factor in these formations. The aquifer under the ranch is a separate adjacent and smaller aquifer. Therefore there may be a cave system formed by water within this aquifer that has yet to be discovered. The discovered caves in the area are very shallow. There are bound to be cave systems deeper within the earth. Therefore, as the water levels shrink and the aquifers dry up, we may discover an entire network of caves that we never knew existed. Hmm, just something to think about. Even if we discover there are no cave formations underground beneath the ranch, all the other caves are relatively close. We basically live on the edge of a cave system created by fault lines and the Edwards Plateau and a very large water system responsible for creating the caves. Now with the visit from a cave dwelling bat, we can conclude that there must be a cave closer to the ranch, and that the ranch is much closer to the cave system then I had previously suspected.

I also researched rainfall totals and river systems in the area, and I noticed that just within miles of the ranch we have a river four miles to the north and two miles to the south. Then I noticed a much larger river system in the county with multiple rivers crisscrossing the entire county. In New Mexico it is a known fact that the black bears use the river systems as passage ways. In Raton New Mexico, bears can often be seen walking in the canals below street level. So could it be that the Sasquatches are using these river systems as their own super highway? Remember this detail about river systems as super highways. I have another story to tell you in my short stories series, which explores this theory.

So, that is as far as my research went, most of the information can be found on the USGS website. I do believe that if they were choosing to hide, this is where they could go to hide. No, not the discovered caves frequented by tourists, but the ones we have not discovered. I am not saying they live in caves. I offer this up as another explanation, as just another place for them to possibly hide and seek refuge.

Chapter Five
What Does A Squatch Say?

Hind sight is 20/20. Now looking back I can sit here and calmly explain what took me two years to understand. It was the small things. These are the things that go unnoticed. That is how they survive. They are so subtle and quiet, and do small things that no one notices, for example gifting rocks, and "borrowing" tools. Then like the many previous renters, when something noticeable happens, people just up and leave without attempting to find out the truth. The experience is forever engrained in their minds and imaginations and described as one of sheer terror. Unfortunately, most people have a five second life altering experience with a Bigfoot/Sasquatch and never return to the site where it happened, and never have another experience. Can you imagine how many people take those terrifying five seconds of their life and allow it to define the entire Bigfoot/Sasquatch experience? For those of us who live in an established habituation site, I can guarantee that we are having more than a five second encounter. We may be having a five second encounter and/or experience every twenty four hours. We notice the little things, and they mean a lot. This is how we are figuring things out. This is where the evidence is coming from and the documentation to substantiate and prove and explain the existence of Bigfoot. You can't prove much if it only happens once and you know nothing about the area, habitat, environment and previous experiences. It is impossible to collect any information that way, let alone analyze the data and come to any meaningful intelligent conclusions.

I find it hilarious when I read about a sighting someone had, and then an "expert researcher" takes up the case and goes to the same location, sometimes years after a sighting, and gives his "expert" opinion and tells the people whether they had a Bigfoot encounter or not. What I love about living here on the ranch is that we have consistency. We can document, and make conclusions. We have created a baseline which allows us to make comparisons during times of activity and times when there is a lack of activity. Looking across this spectrum after two years allows me the ability to pick out certain patterns of behavior, predict encounters, and make conclusions based on our ongoing experiences. Here is one tiny detail that we didn't realize was happening to us. Now that we know, it makes you wonder if they have a sense of humor, and it makes you wonder about their intellectual capabilities.

Many times during the last two years since we moved to the ranch, the kids would come running down the stairs yelling, "Yes ma'am, did you call me?" This got so exhausting and frustrating that I would yell at my kids. See, when I really needed them and I hollered up the stairs, they could not hear me. So, what's up? How are they able to hear these phantom disembodied voices all the time, yet they can't hear me when it is chore time? It took two years to figure this out. I was so frustrated that my kids couldn't even call my name without me snapping back at them. I am embarrassed to admit it, but this has put us all on edge.

Don't get mad at me, I am only human. My human instincts take over just like everyone else's. When you do not understand and cannot explain it, you tend to get extremely frustrated.

Then I read that one book which described a habituation situation that also involved children. That experience also took place somewhere in Texas. One of the common experiences was identical to mine. The children began to hear someone or something calling them by name, and usually it was not their mother, even though the children were 100% sure it was their mother.

Just recently one of my boys came running down stairs. The boys had been in bed upstairs fast asleep for quite some time. My oldest asked if I had called them, and I said, "no, of course not". Then my son said, "I swear it was you mom, it sounded like your angry voice!" Oh, that did it! I am so embarrassed to admit this, but the Sasquatches know how to mimic momma's angry voice! That is mind boggling and freaking hilarious. Do you realize what that means? So, do you realize the level of understanding they must have and the communication capabilities, not to mention their sense of humor? See, I used to laugh at Bobo when he would make Bigfoot calls trying to mimic the Sasquatches on television. Now I laugh just envisioning the Sasquatches mimicking Mama Sullivan on the Bigfoot Ranch. Yikes! I am not sure which one is funnier.

Yes, it turns out that Bigfoot/Sasquatches have the ability to speak, and yes they also have the ability to mimic us. I knew they were able to mimic birds, I even got caught up in a mimicking game one day in early 2012. I couldn't tell who was mocking who at first. Like a fool I just kept whistling back until I realized it must have been a Squatch. This went on for about fifteen minutes. They must have thought I was so stupid. "Watch me make the hairless one whistle like a bird." Oh they must have had so much fun with me those first two years. Well now I am going to have fun back. They are not going to put one over on me again. I am now actively trying to communicate with the Sasquatches, with the help and advice of others with vocalization experiences. I am determined to get down to the bottom of this and explore the depths of their communication abilities.

It turns out that these creatures that others are

deciding to call animals and apes not only have the ability to mimic human speech, but they also know what the words mean. Why is it that Zack comes running down the stairs and says someone is calling him and he assumes it is me calling out his name. Is it ironic or just coincidental that during these times Kirk is at Karate? How did the Squatch know that the word Zack matches up with my son Zack? Not only that, my kids say when "I" am calling them, it sounds just like me. They are 100% convinced it is me calling them from downstairs. This happens all the time.

There have been times when the kids are outside and they hear me calling, and I am inside working on the computer. You can't hear me calling from inside the house. This used to happen all the time when we first moved to the ranch. The boys would hear me calling them when they were playing outside. This is the one experience that we can proclaim is consistent. It continues till this day. It is non-threatening and communicative in nature. Just a few weeks ago as Zack was feeding the dogs in the morning before heading off to school, he got in the van and looked at me and said someone yelled at him and said, "hey!" Then he clearly heard his name. My boys don't get scared, because they haven't been taught to be scared. This is all new to us and I am therefore trying to teach my sons not to fear the unknown. If anything they are fascinated and accepting of these new experiences. I don't want them to fear what we cannot explain and understand. I want them to learn to accept it and then try to figure it out from a logical rational place, not from a fearful place.

When Daphne was here for the summer, she thought she was having paranormal experiences because something kept calling Da Ph A Neee.......In other words, someone is having a field day calling my kids by their names. She is older than the boys and has already been programed by society that this is "paranormal", not normal. Yet the boys haven't learned that yet, and they think it is rather normal. Do you realize what that means? They know our names. What was unusual at the time is that I could not hear their names being called. My husband and I were downstairs in bed reading our books, everyone was out for the night and then Kirk comes stomping downstairs again because we had yelled out his name. You should have seen the look on his face. He was serious. Someone had called out in such a way that he thought it was an emergency, which is why he ran downstairs. My husband and I just gasped with our mouths wide open, because we had heard absolutely nothing. This led me to consider the possibility that the Squatches were communicating with my kids using nonverbal communication skills. Yes, I know what you are going to say. Get over it!! Quit acting like that is so paranormal and never heard of. I spent two whole months researching for this book, and ended up not using any of it in the book. I know there are people that don't want to hear it, and I really don't care to preach it either. I also know there are those of you who know exactly what I am talking about. For those of you who don't know, let me just say this. We use several forms of nonverbal communication in our everyday lives. It is quite normal. Some of us are more sensitive to this form of communication than others. As a mother, my children rarely cried the first few years of their lives. They didn't have to, I was aware of their needs before they had a chance to cry and communicate that to me. I just found that to be so normal. As an educator with graduate studies in language acquisition, I know what I am talking about. Also as a teacher, and a mother, you learn to read your kids. I can answer questions just by making eye contact with my students at school and with my kids at home. It blows them away every time. I can also tell when people are lying. There is a science to reading nonverbal cues and having the ability to read people telepathically. Many individuals in law enforcement, psychiatry and psychology can attest to the realities of telepathic communication abilities. So there it is, wake up or grow up. There is no debate. It has been researched, studied, documented, verified and proven.

I did read an article while I was researching the topic of telepathy among the Bigfoot/Sasquatches, in which a self-proclaimed researcher/expert/anthropologist/cryptozoologist, went out into the woods and sat there to see if "they" would speak to her. She sat there on a log for a while and then declared it must not be true because they didn't talk to her. Oh My God! I have to stop right here and take a deep breath. I want to insert so many sarcastic remarks, but I must refrain. My momma raised me better. My daddy also didn't raise a fool, apparently hers did. So, because "I can't hear it, it didn't happen, doesn't exist and can't possibly be true?" There are so many philosophical arguments that I researched, but I do not want to spiral out of control down that black hole again. All I can say is that this falls under

"The argument that appeals to ignorance." Like I always say, "You can't argue with stupid!" (Sorry I just couldn't help myself!)

So, yes, back to the subject at hand. They do have this ability. Call it whatever you want. I call it communication. There are those of us who have the ability to listen and hear them. Not all humans are capable of such perception and sensitivity. I had always wondered why I could hear stuff all the time. I had wondered why I had been so hypersensitive to noises out on the ranch. I have always been. I remember for the first year and a half I would wake up in the middle of the night. I would jump out of bed and run to the windows and look outside. The only way I could describe it was that I just knew someone was out there. I felt it and yes I somehow heard it. It sounded like unintelligible chattering inside my head. Then one night, I heard a voice that was so loud and so strong, that I responded back in my sleep. I yelled out "WHAT" and nearly knocked my husband right out of bed. I knew at that minute they were talking to my children using telepathy. Two weeks later it happened to my husband as well, he yelled out and nearly knocked me out of bed. I realized then that the Sasquatches have the ability to speak to someone directly. Therefore, only Zack heard them when they were talking to Zack. Kirk heard them when they were talking to Kirk and no one else. I was the only one to hear them when someone yelled at me. It is quite an experience.

This has become such a normal part of our everyday lives. Just recently when someone yelled out to me, and I was standing there with the utter look of shock and terror in my eyes, and then looked at my kids and asked, "Did you just hear that?" Kirk my youngest just comes over, puts his little hand on my shoulder, leans his head to the right and says, "Mom, maybe they are a just talking to you in your head, it happens to me all the time." He wasn't kidding, just the week before, someone woke Kirk up at 11p.m. According to Kirk, someone told him to get up and look outside the window. His room is on the second floor just above the patio. He got up out of bed, he had to open the heavy wooden blinds to look out of his bedroom window. He came tearing down the stairs to our bedroom and yelled for us to look outside. The wood pile had caught on fire and was engulfed in flames. When I asked him how he knew to look outside, he just honestly and innocently looked at me and said, "Duh, they told me." Do you realize what this means? They kept our house from going up in flames, and possibly prevented a catastrophic forest fire like the one we had in Bastrop two years ago. I thank God every day for our Sasquatches.

I realize that not everyone has this ability to communicate nonverbally. I have always considered it a curse. I don't enjoy reading people's thoughts. It can be quite intrusive and burdensome. Due to our experiences on the ranch, I soon began to realize that my children must also be hypersensitive since they seem to have the ability to hear disembodied voices as well as thoughts. It was time for me to accept the truth, about myself, my history, and my heritage. Since after all it seems my children have inherited my God given traits and abilities. This may also help explain why I could possibly be having these amazing Bigfoot/Sasquatch experiences. No, I am not crazy. No I do not have a family history of mental illness. What I do have is a long rich Native American History from both sides of the family. Most notably my maternal Great Grandmother was a healer, a medicine woman, or in some circles, a curandera, or a shaman.

My Great Grandmother was known in our German community for being a healer, an herbalist, and a midwife. She delivered all of her grandchildren and some of her great grandchildren before me. I was born in the local county hospital. My doctor who delivered me, was the local family doctor. Even he knew of my little old Native American Great Grandmother. There were many times I was told, that he had referred a few patients to her, and vice versa. My experiences with her were limited to the occasional chamomile teas and massages to relieve my pain. She also prayed over me for healing, which we call laying on of hands. She was an upstanding Christian woman and a devout Catholic who always sat on the front row every Sunday morning.

It wasn't until I was much older that I realized she had "other" abilities that we never mentioned, talked about, or acknowledged. I was not taught, nor was I trained by her. We spoke completely different languages. She was a lovely little Native American Woman, and I was a long haired pony tailed little Texan. I had no idea we were even Native American. It was as though I was being raised so far away from the truth, my heritage, and my true identity. It really didn't matter, she came to me in my dreams and spoke to me often. I also believe she passed on many of her abilities to me, and then I passed them on to all of my children. No, they are not supernatural powers. I see it as more of an awareness of nature, my environment and all those around me. This is why I believe Daphene knew, and heard them when we first moved to the ranch. She was so aware that something and someone was out there. It also explains how, at the very beginning, they were able to talk to my boys as they played outside, and my boys could hear them and clearly understand them. I also believe this is why they are attracted to us and we are so accepting of them. It all makes perfect sense. I do believe it has taken us time to get to know them and the same amount of time for them to get to know us.

So during this time of mutual attraction and understanding, we just learned to accept what was happening here on the ranch. I do believe that once the Sasquatches realized I could hear their thoughts and I could hear them at night, all the "chatter" stopped. I even remember the night it happened. It was in June of 2013. I was waiting for some kind of confirmation that the

Bigfoot/Sasquatches were still on or near the ranch after the hog hunts were over. I waited and waited. I slept with the windows open looking and listening for a sign. It finally happened. I remember waking up in the middle of the night and hearing a conversation between two individuals. I knew instinctively it was a Mama Sasquatch scolding her baby. See, the mama never comes around. We have had the Big Daddy, the Juvy and the Baby come close to the house, I mean in the yard and on the roof. That close. I believe this was the first time the Mama came for a visit. In my opinion she was furious with the younger ones since they just walked right up to the property. I still believe she was shocked that they, without hesitation and without fear and trepidation walked right up to the house. She let her young ones know that this was unacceptable. I heard her voice, not telepathically, but physically heard her voice out loud. I also heard the baby's voice. Mama Sasquatch is quieter and has a softer tone and voice than Big Daddy has. Also, she did not smell as the Big Daddy does. She was gentle in her tone yet very forceful. I did not hear her footsteps, or foot stomps. I held my breath so I could take in every word they were saying. I closed my eyes so I could hear with my ears, my brain and my heart. The words they used were short. I heard only monosyllabic words. I want to say and believe that they sounded almost Native American, but after spending time on an Apache Indian reservation and having my son in a Bilingual Apache class, it did not sound native. The Native American languages sound more relaxed with more of an emphasis on the beginning of the word. My honest opinion is that it sounded more like Chinese. Very high pitched and fast. I laid there in my bed with the windows open and listened in on this conversation between two Sasquatches. I tried to take in every single word. I searched for meaning and understanding, but I could not decipher this new language. I did understand the tone and the intent, and mother to mother, I knew someone was in trouble. The conversation abruptly stopped, as I believe she realized I could hear every word. I believe she heard my thoughts. This was the moment they realized I could hear them. They must be used to the fact that most humans are unaware of them and unable to see or hear them. This was the moment they knew I could understand them. It was at this moment the conversation and the chatter on the ranch ended. It was after this evening that I truly began to sleep through the night after living on the ranch for eighteen months. I was exhausted. I finally had complete silence. I could finally rest. It would be another nine months till I heard them speak again, and this time it was directly to me.

One day on my way to work I had a rather funny experience. I realized, not only do they know our names, they have quite a sense of humor. This happened just days after a fellow "Knower" known as Sasquatch Ontario, or Mike Paterson had suggested that I go outside and begin to communicate with them. He suggested I pat my chest and declare my name out loud. I did. I continued by pointing out other objects and stating their names as well. This was going to be the beginning of my attempts at Sasquatch communication. I felt as though I was following in the footsteps of Diane Fossey(1932-85) The only problem is that I wasn't ready for it. It took her months and months to establish a relationship with the mountain gorillas, and years of research. I wasn't ready for a response! I was just getting comfortable with the whole idea of standing on my back porch and communicating with someone out in the woods. Then, just one day later I heard the loudest attempt at a vocalization. It sounded like the huge 3000 pound bull outside in the pasture trying to talk to me, near my bedroom window. Yes, I freaked out!! My ears weren't ready to hear that. It was just unbelievable and unimaginable. I really did not expect a response, nor did I expect it that quickly. I know it wasn't the bull, it was a male Sasquatch. His voice and tone is that deep and sounds similar to the bull, yet this voice was trying to pronounce sounds. I was elated and terrified all at the same time, if that makes any sense at all. I asked for it, then I cowered. I tried to keep my wits about me and use all of my knowledge of Language Acquisition. How lucky was I that I had taken this graduate level course in graduate school. I knew what to expect. I knew it would be extremely difficult for a person or creature to attempt to vocalize for the first time. I know I reacted poorly, and hoped they would give me another opportunity, and they did. It happened the very next day.

I was preparing to go to work the very next day, when as I jumped in my car and began to drive off down the driveway, I heard "NO, Ssssssuuuussss". I knew instinctively that someone was trying to communicate with me, and I knew it wasn't the bull, he was nowhere in sight. It was the same voice from the day before. I was shocked. I tried so hard not to react negatively again. I had to place it out of my mind and tuck it somewhere in my brain so that I could continue to function. I had to drive to work. Then when I had the time and space to analyze what I had heard, I busted out laughing. I replayed it in my head over and over again, NO Sssssuusss, with emphasis on the ss. What was he or she trying to tell me? I thought "Oh My God they are finally trying to tell me something." "Quick get a notebook!" "It might be profound." "It might be the answer to all of the mysteries behind Bigfoot!" Then I realized what someone was trying to say to me. I sat there and rolled my eyes and looked to the high heavens. "Really?" No, it wasn't the key to unlock all the mysteries of the universe therefore creating peace and harmony and universal understanding and acceptance. No. He or She said, "Not Susan"! Ha, ha, ha, ha! How funny. Someone has a sense of humor. See, Susan is my pen name. It is not my real name!! They know that too!! I know it sounds crazy and yes unbelievable. I cannot explain this, I am just recounting my experiences. "Not Susan!" I know for a fact they have a sense of humor! I am guessing the response was from the Juvy Sasquatch. Is that not just like a goofball teenager, always joking around? You see what all you ape chasers are missing out on? As I was standing there on my back porch patting my chest, I gave them my real name. There was no need to lie to the

Bigfoot/Sasquatches and give them my pen name, Susan.
Yet, somehow they know I am not using my real name. I bet
they also know the reason why. It is to keep them safe from
harm, and to keep crazy hunters away from the property.
So, just as I have gone to great lengths to keep their babies
and family safe, they have returned the favor by keeping my
babies and family safe, by waking my son up and telling him
the patio was on fire. This is the moment I break into tears
and realize how truly important, and profound our
relationship has become.

This is also the moment I thank God for the human
relationships I have developed. During each event that had
happened I immediately emailed my new friend from Ohio,
Mark. He was with me every step of the way. I couldn't run
to the neighbors or go to work and tell everyone what had
just happened, and besides who would believe me? I thank
God for the group of "Knowers" and "Believers" who are
emerging from all of this. We are not part of the "Bigfoot
Community". We are just individuals who are speaking our
truth. That is all, yet there seems to be a vocal majority who
seems to be threatened by our knowledge, our experiences
and our truths. I am also grateful to Mike Paterson, who

took the time to email me and gave me advice and the support I needed to continue reaching out to the Bigfoot/Sasquatches.

Susan Sullivan

Chapter Six
Defending Mike

Speaking of Mike, let me tell you the story of how we met. One day I had a twitter follower named Mark from Ohio, who began to email me. He is someone I now consider my lifelong friend and confidant. We email each other weekly and sometimes daily. There are those days when I am experiencing ongoing Bigfoot activity and our communication escalates and we go back and forth minute by minute. It was Mark who sent me a link of Sasquatch Ontario and asked me to review the video/audio footage. He wanted to know my honest opinion. Was it real, or a fake? I had never heard of this individual, so I listened to the audio for the first time without any preconceived ideas of what I was about to hear. When I heard the audio I felt something inside me that came from the depths of my soul. I had heard that before. As an educator I have been in a special education classroom, and I have heard a student speak with the exact same monologue. I have heard the same repetitive words, because that is all they know. It is the beginning of speech. It is called Echolalia, a subject echoes what he is being taught. It is easily recognized by repetitive unintelligible speech. It seems meaningful to us because we place meaning to it. I have seen other students come into the classroom and scream with delight when the special education student responded with "I love you!" The students assume it is intelligible, meaningful language, not realizing it is just repetitive speech. The most familiar words I recognized immediately were the "one, two, three" and "flower". I heard on the audio. Those are usually the first words we teach after our names. One two three, are so easy and basic and easy to remember and repeat and only one syllable. It is a song, with no meaning. What stirred my soul was that these words came from a Bigfoot/Sasquatch, which Mike refers to as the Ancient Ones. Not once did I conclude this audio was a fake. I did however recognize this as someone's attempt at speech, not necessarily communication, but an honest attempt at speech with the intent to communicate. He has to learn how to speak our language before he can communicate verbally and intelligently.

Everyone begins to speak this way, we just don't pay much attention to it, since we continue to develop cognitively and verbally. We just forget how we sounded at that stage. But, there are those unique individuals who age physically, but not cognitively and not developmentally and therefore their communication skills do not develop either. We think it is cute when they are little, but it is quite distinct when you hear an adult speak with the developmental age of an eighteen month old.

I bring this video/audio up because I am taking a stand here. I have come to know Mike through emails, and I would like to defend him by defending his evidence. I have seen the other videos of various people who counter his claims. There are even a few "self-proclaimed" experts who have christened themselves as the demigods of the Bigfoot Community. They have come out against Mike Paterson solely on the basis that they have not had the same experience, therefore he has to be lying. That is definitely an argument that appeals to ignorance. So, when you hear these people make these statements, they are truly displaying their ego and their ignorance. Since they did not have that experience, you didn't either. How juvenile, no how infantile.

Then I read and heard another argument in an interview that since Mike did not allow anyone onto the property to check it out, he must be lying. Once again, it was a self-ordained internet personality and camp counselor who has placed himself high up on a pedestal. He thinks he needs his Bigfoot expertise to validate Mike's claims. I have not let any researchers on the ranch either. I have had three researchers ask, and I have refused. I don't need anyone telling me what I did or did not see. I don't need anyone validating or invalidating my personal experiences. I did share however, a lovely afternoon with author Rob Riggs discussing and comparing our similar experiences.

I am not defending Mike and his evidence based on our friendship, or our common Bigfoot experiences, I am defending it based on my education alone.

I had seen a video of another "expert". He claimed to be a "Bigfoot Audio Specialist". He had all the equipment which he used to take apart Mike's audio to prove Mike and the property owner were fakes. My nephew owns audio equipment, maybe we should call him an expert. Also this guy is taking apart audio of a recording from YouTube. He does his best to debunk and disprove but offers nothing to further the understanding of Bigfoot. I don't believe he is an expert in linguistics, foreign languages, or dialects or language acquisition. He is an expert in audio equipment.

So, I am however going to claim my expertise based on my Graduate Studies in Education, more specifically Language Acquisition, and Bilingual Education as well as Multicultural Education. To break it down even further, this is the study, research and understanding as to how one acquires language, both first language and subsequent languages as well as new cultures. There are well established documented levels of language development. I am explaining and analyzing the audio based on fundamental documented processes necessary when acquiring a new language. The "audio/equipment specialist" based his accusations on what he heard on the YouTube audio and his dislike for Mike, not on some knowledge or actual expertise. He knew nothing about the cognitive, developmental aspects of language acquisition or the physiological effects of acquiring a new language and new culture.

In Mike's video I heard an individual speaking on the audio, mimicking what he had learned. If this equipment operator had studied anything about language, he would have realized he made a total fool of himself. The first claim is that Nephatia, the subject on the audio, sounds exactly like the owner. Surprise surprise! When I taught my first class in Bilingual Education, my angry mentor was furious because my cute little Spanish speaking first graders suddenly began to speak English with a Texas Twang, just like me. Yup, twenty four six year olds sounded just like me. They took on my dialect, my mannerisms, my habits, and pauses in speech, even my laugh. The girls started to wear their hair long and flick it back just like me. This is called imitation, and it is part of the process of acquiring a new language. This is also part of cultural acquisition, which I also studied in my Multicultural Education Graduate Level class. You mimic your teacher. Nephatia met and knew the

owner before ever meeting Mike, therefore, he was
mimicking the owner, and it only makes sense that he would
sound exactly like the owner. He wasn't going to sound like
Sean Connery with a British accent. Also, remember what
my kids said? The voices they are hearing on the ranch
sound exactly like mine, not Julia Childs. They are mimicking
me. Why not, they are observing me all the time. I know
this is going to shock some of you, but I am also the loudest
and the most flamboyant personality on the ranch. Of
course they are going to sound like me. God help us if they
start cursing! Let me just go ahead and apologize to
humanity for teaching Bigfoot his first curse words.

The speech in the Sasquatch Ontario audio was very
basic because acquiring a new language is very difficult.
That is why Nephatia sounds the way he does. I once met
an international businessman, Mr. Nakagami, during a
young political leadership program at SMU. He was Asian.
He explained to our group that learning English was very
difficult for first language Asian speakers. We use distinctly
different parts of our mouths and throats to form our words.
It is utterly exhausting and sometimes painful. That is why I
believe you hear that pain in Nepahtia's voice. He was really

trying hard to speak. Mr. Nakagami also claimed it could take up to ten years for a first language Asian speaker to fully acquire English. It does require many years of careful observation and mimicry. The languages are just that different. I mentioned this because I believe the Sasquatches first language is very similar to Chinese. How do I know this? Well, because I heard them speak in my own backyard just outside my bedroom window that night in June of 2013.

I have heard the Sierra Sounds, and ours sound nothing like that. So, apparently the Bigfoot/Sasquatches have different regional dialects. I think our Texas Sasquatches speak kind of slow and maybe with a Sasquatchy Twang. (Just Kidding!) The Sierra Sounds audio was so fast they had to slow it down to hear the language. Ours did not speak that fast. I could clearly hear a language, some was monosyllabic, and some polysyllabic with syllables and pauses in the language, and emphasis on distinct syllables. I was able to hear them with my own ears.

What Mike captured on audio was a gold mine. We have a chance to truly communicate with these creatures, but no we apparently prefer to knock on trees as our form of communication. Why isn't anyone studying this? Why instead do we have jealous individuals attacking one another?

The audio that Mike has acquired should be held up and scientifically reviewed. This is the first documented evidence of a Sasquatch speaking English. Instead of tearing him down, people should acknowledge or at least allow for the possibility that this creature was attempting to learn English and attempting to communicate. This should be studied and hailed as ground breaking, but Nephatia's voice has fallen on deaf ears.

Chapter Seven

Skinny Dipping Bigfoot

Summer school was finally over. (This is a repeat of the short stories book Memories) I could finally enjoy the summer at home with my kids on the ranch. Summers in July are unbearably hot. This July was no exception. It was terribly hot. We did not dare go to the pond this year. Everyone, from Austin to Houston was reporting unusual snake activity. They could only stay dormant for so long during the drought from the previous year. It was time for them to come out. I had spotted a huge brown water moccasin in a makeshift damn that I had created during the day of Daphene's graduation celebration. My brother had come down from Dallas and I walked him to the pond. I wanted him to give me some tips on how to create and stabilize the small dam. I did not want the new fish I had just stocked in the pond to swim to the marshy area. I wanted them to stay in the pond. So, as we stood there overlooking the makeshift dam, we saw the largest snake slither through the logs. It was huge. It was larger in diameter than my fat forearms. I never saw the tail end of the water moccasin. That was all I needed. We did not spend one day in the pond during the summer. Water moccasins are known to be very aggressive and territorial, and this year they were worse. I have heard stories of water moccasins chasing people. I had a good friend tell me how they came out of her pond and made their way to the house and stood guard outside in the shade near the water faucets. I was terrified of the water moccasins.

The copperheads were equally dangerous. The difference with copperheads is they do not just hang out near ponds and lakes. They are everywhere. There is this cute little bakery eighteen miles down the highway to the north. I went there one day to buy the kids some cookies after school. The elderly woman there had told us that her husband was in ICU. He had been bitten by a baby copperhead while changing a tire.

My husband's colleague at work was bitten by a copperhead at his ranch and was also in the hospital. Then, later my very own neighbor to the north just beyond the cattle guard had been bitten by a copperhead in his garden. That was just too risky. So, I kept the boys indoors and we stayed away from the pond.

They really love to swim, so I bought them a twelve foot round and three foot deep blue pool with an inflatable ring at the top to hold it up. It sat nicely on the huge cement back porch right next to the sliding patio doors. I could keep an eye on my boys at all times. We cleaned off the porch and set out a new blue tarp underneath the new pool. I inflated the ring that sits around the top edge. I set up the filter system and we were good to go. My boys were elated!! They absolutely loved the idea of having a pool right outside the back door. They would wake up in the morning and spend all day in the pool. We bought balls, water guns, toys, rings, and noodles. We only had the pool for two days when the kids began to notice something strange was going on, again it didn't take but a few days for the activity to begin. My boys said that when they came downstairs in the morning just two days after setting up the pool, they noticed all the pool toys were gone. The inflatable ball was missing, and the blue football was outside the pool about twenty feet away. We were very curious. Then Zack mentioned that he also saw hair in the pool that morning. He checked the filter and showed me the hair. I also noticed grass or hay in with the hair. None of us had been out in the pasture. The two dogs we had were too small to get into the pool and were too scared to go near the pool. Our other dog had unfortunately been killed by a passing car on the highway. The yard is a well-kept manicured lawn with short green grass, no straw, or hay. We all knew what was happening. All I could think of was what that Juvy Squatch must think of my boys dunking themselves in this blue pool. They would stay in there for hours. Hey, he had to try it out too! And I guess he did! We all laughed when we visualized him skinny dipping in the pool at night.

One day I had asked Zack to top off the pool with water. He turned the water on, but forgot to turn it off. So that night I went to sleep, and sometime around 2:30 a.m., I woke up. I do not know why I woke up. As I said before, I became hyper sensitive. I knew something was outside and I heard it. I think I felt and sensed someone out there who was agitated. I instinctively got up out of bed and headed for the bathroom. I normally turn on the light to the bathroom, but this night I did not. I looked out the bathroom window which faces the backyard and I saw a black fury creature lurking on the other side of the chain link fence. It was on all fours. Its' rear end was sticking straight up in the air. I knew that was not a coyote, it was too long and its rear was too high, and its legs were too long and straight. It basically looked like an awkward teenager playing twister. It took me about five seconds to play out all the possibilities in my head. The first one was coyote, No! The next was cougar, No! Then wild hog, No! Then wild dog, No! It had to be the Juvy Squatch. He was standing with his head down. Then I realized he was pacing. He kept moving from side to side as if he was agitated, and then he kept going back to this one spot by the fence, and then he left. I believe he realized I was watching him. He came back one last time and headed out into the woods. I knew exactly what I saw and I knew exactly who it was. There was no question in my mind I had just seen the Juvy Squatch. The backyard is lit up by a street light out back. Every ranch has a light that automatically comes on at night. So, that explains how I clearly saw him.

I could not wait for daylight. I was going to look for tracks and evidence. When I opened the sliding glass door I realized why he was pacing and why he was so concerned. Zack had left the water on. It was pouring out of the pool, onto the lawn towards the huge cement bird bath and down towards the fence and down the hill into the woods. The spot where the Juvy stood by the fence was exactly where the water made a small stream downhill. I looked for tracks, but there were just too many leaves. I drew a picture of what I had seen that night the very next day. I knew this was the same Juvy Squatch we had seen in the tree near the cattle guard the year before. He looks like a skinny teenager covered in black fur. He is probably six feet tall. Not well developed at all. He has not matured yet and does not have the big muscles and extremely large dimensions that his father has. I am going to make a wild proclamation here. I think he hangs out at our place quite often. He seems rather comfortable around our house.

I had a researcher ask me further details about the Juvy Squatch I had seen that night. Here is what I told him. It stood awkwardly. It was not on its knees. It had its head to the ground as if it was sniffing the ground for something. The legs were straight, therefore the rear end stuck up in the air. I immediately took to the internet and found a similar picture to what I had seen that night. It is the picture of the Pennsylvania Game Trail Camera shot of a Juvenile. That is a perfect depiction of what I had seen that night. Unmistakable!

I was not afraid and neither were the kids. It was as if we already knew he was hanging out at our place. He is also that keenly aware of what my boys are doing, again, and obviously watching them. First it was basketball, now it is swimming. That just sounds so normal. We basically have a nosey neighborhood kid who comes over to our yard quite often and checks out our pool and plays with my kids' toys at night. Like I said, it just sounds so normal.

The boys continued to play in the pool every single day. That is until the one day we were invited to go swimming with a church group out of town. I was asked to help a mom who was taking a group of twenty kids to the city pool in the next town. The church rented a bus and we all hopped on and left for the entire day. We had a great time. When we got back we were shocked to find something had damaged the pool. The ring was deflated and half the water was pouring out of the pool. I wondered if he was upset that we were gone. I wondered if he was counting on watching my boys play in the pool as they had done every single day, except that day. We never blamed the dogs. Pickles, our new dog is a fifteen pound Terrier who could never reach the ring three and a half feet up where the ring was compromised. Wendy is fifty five pounds, but she never went near the pool. She was afraid the boys would throw her in, and besides she never seemed interested in the pool. She never even went to the back porch while we had the pool. She stayed in the front yard, and avoided the back of the house as long as the pool was there. There was only one creature on the ranch who seemed interested in the pool and that was the Juvy Squatch. So, that was it for the pool. It was destroyed and we could not use it again. The boys and I spent the rest of the summer at Daphne's in Dallas. We still had our house there and she was attending college in the area. I enrolled the boys in swim lessons at the local junior college where they had a huge Olympic sized pool. We swam at the local water park and never thought about the pool again. Dad met up with us the first week of August and we left for our vacation in Hawaii. Again we were leaving the ranch behind.

No we did not keep the hair and submit it for DNA analysis. Even though I thought it was evidence, it was not reliable scientific evidence. There are too many animals on the ranch to conclude that the hair samples in the pool belonged to a Juvy Squatch or a Baby Squatch. Hair flies away very easily. It also looked much like the lint you peel off the drier screen from the drier vent, which also comes out black and gray due to a combination of colors. I had to address this since a reader could not understand why I did not collect the specimen and submit it for analysis. I am very careful and analytical. I do not jump to conclusions easily. I am describing what we saw in the pool, and made these conclusions based on circumstantial evidence, (the missing toys) and later eyewitness evidence (my sighting). At the time, I had no idea there was ongoing research and DNA studies going on right here in Texas. Had I known, I might have collected the hair samples and submitted them.

I had also collected a stool sample as well with pictures. I had bagged and tagged it and placed it on a shelf in the garage in case a researcher ever asked for it, but it later disappeared.

Here are those pictures:

Figure 3 Scat found in 2012.

Figure 4 Scat found in 2012.

These are the pictures of scat we collected the first year. We found this scat within the first few months outside on the driveway. We really knew what we had the second we walked outside. With all the activity around the house, and the fact that Daphene had already found a very large sampling of scat on the roof, we were able to come to certain conclusions.

I had a Bigfoot researcher from a Texas Bigfoot Group ask me, "What made me think it was Bigfoot scat?" Well, first of all It made perfect sense. We were expecting to see evidence, since we had so much activity in the first few months on the ranch. Second, it was smaller than the cows and did not look at all lIke the dog poop. Third, I noticed a very small hole poked into the scat on the lower left side. It was a smooth hole that looked as though it was made by a tiny finger. I believe it was made by a Baby Bigfoot. Just like our babies, they are curious and tend to poke at their poop too! Also, during the third year, I found tiny fingerprints on the barbeque grill, that I believe were made by a baby. The finger prints are so tiny, which lead me to believe that they were made by a similar sized creature.

www.texasbigfootinmybackyard.com

Chapter Eight
Big Daddy Spotted

When the new school year began I was ready to share the finished product with my students. Word soon got around that I had written a Bigfoot book. Yes, there were many skeptics, and that is okay. I had no intentions of shoving this information down anyone's throat. Many of the students started to share their own experiences and stories with me. I listened with an open mind and an open heart. One student who lived maybe five miles away had mentioned seeing something in the tree line that stood above the fence. She instinctively knew what it was. It was as though she was finally able to acknowledge what she had known all along. She seemed relieved.

Big Daddy Crossing a Bridge

Another student stopped me in the hall one day and said her mother wanted to tell me something. "Okay" I said. She then proceeded with her mother's account from the previous weekend. Her mother was driving north on a highway when she had an encounter with a 10 ft. tall black hairy creature. He was so close, that she slammed on the brakes. She claims she could see the whites of his eyes. That was how close she was. When I asked exactly where this encounter took place, they had no way of knowing exactly where I lived. I work in a neighboring county and no one knows where the ranch is located. Her mother happened to be driving down the highway within two miles from the ranch. She was crossing a bridge over a creek that winds its way to the ranch. I believe she had an encounter with our Big Daddy. When she got home, she began to describe her terrifying experience to her family. Her daughter knew immediately who she was describing. She was talking about our Big Daddy. Her mother at first thought her family would think she was crazy, but she was greatly relieved when her daughter began to identify the creature and gave it a name, which gave her mother the validation she was searching for.

Hog Hunting and Bigfoot

Several months later while I was at the High School campus just walking down the hall minding my own business, I had a six foot tall teenager dressed head to toe in camouflage, ready for hunting. He grabbed my arm turning me around right where I stood and asked, "Are you the one who saw Bigfoot?" You should have seen the look on his face. I knew he was dead serious. I gave him my time and my undivided attention. He recounted his story from a recent hunting experience that had occurred that very weekend. This one took place thirty miles to the north of us. He said that he and five other buddies were hog hunting at night. They had spot lights, shot guns, and cellphones with camera capabilities. He said they were near a pond. They were shining a light on a huge bush where they heard and had seen some movement. They were all looking in the direction of the bush, which was near a pond, when this huge 10 ft. tall male creature stood up from behind the bush. He just stared at the boys. He said even though they had rifles, shot guns, and cellphones, they were all frozen with fear, right where they stood. No one took a shot, and no one took a picture, they were that paralyzed with shock and with fear. I believed every word he said. You should have seen the look of relief on his face when I said, "Yes, that is our Big Daddy." I always validate their sightings with, "I believe you". I find that is all people want and need to hear.

I soon realized I wasn't having to convince anyone about the possible existence of Bigfoot/Sasquatch on the ranch. People within a thirty mile radius were telling me about their very own Bigfoot encounters. I was just the one validating and identifying what people already knew was out there and had already seen. They were just too afraid to put a name to it.

Two Screams in the Night

Then there was the one day I was at school and another student told me that the Saturday before he had heard something screaming as though it was injured. He said it didn't sound like anything he had ever heard before, but he somehow instinctively knew it was a Bigfoot. It was loud, scared, and definitely injured. He didn't dare go out into the wooded pasture to take a look. I listened to his story and made note of his responses, his demeanor, and his physiological responses. This student is an honor student. I have known him for three years. I absolutely trust and believe every word he said. I took it all in and assessed the whole human response to stress. I knew he was telling me the truth.

The next class period another student, mentioned that on that very same weekend he and his brother were shooting out into the pasture where they lived. This student was not aware that there were any laws on the books concerning guns. He told me several stories that day about selling stolen guns and other illegal behavior he was involved in. He honestly, because of his IQ did not understand the consequences of his actions. Then he began to brag about having shot at a creature he had seen lurking in the shadows. He had no idea what it was, but thought it was funny and cool just shooting randomly into the night. He then described that he knew he had shot the creature because it took off running and screaming into the pasture. He also described a blood curdling scream he had never heard before coming from the injured creature. He tried to convince me that it must have been a cougar. I doubt he was that good of a shot that he could hit a crouching cougar in the dark, he lacked the coordination skills. But, I truly believe he accidentally hit a curious juvenile Bigfoot lurking in the shadows near his house. Now this individual has a lower IQ than the first, maybe thirty points less. Yes, I can assess that as well, since I had a class in that too, Assessments and Diagnostics in Education. I also noted his demeanor.

I tried to explain first, that he needed to discontinue his illegal activities. I continued to explain the legal consequences of his behavior. I also had to explain that selling stolen guns was against the law. I then had to explain that shooting randomly into the dark was dangerous. He looked at me with a blank stare. He was dumbfounded. He could not make the connections between his actions and the possible consequences. Then I tried to explain that he quite possibly shot at a Bigfoot. He could not conceive or comprehend the idea that a creature such as Bigfoot could possibly be out in his pasture. Due to his extremely low IQ he still could not make any of the connections between his behavior and the possible consequences. What if it had been a woman out in the pasture? Then I asked him where he lived. I had an idea already, based on the previous student's claims. He lived just down the highway from the other student, who had heard the screams. This injured creature ran for miles, screaming into the dead of night. In my opinion, apparently this student had unintentionally shot a curious juvenile Bigfoot/Sasquatch, and the second student who lived miles away on a ranch down the highway from this student, heard the screams as it ran through his property. Same time, same night, same sounds, same creature. Two distinctly different reactions based on different levels of understanding, knowledge and IQ.

Captured Bigfoot

Another junior high student had told me that her grandfather had pictures that she had seen long ago. She believed they were pictures of a Bigfoot. Her grandpa hid them under the floor boards of his old farmhouse. He refused to let the grandkids see the pictures again. He did tell his grandchildren several stories, which match up to the story I had been told the previous Christmas about a Bigfoot having been caught and chained up in a barn. I was told that a farmer in our area had caught a Bigfoot, chained it up in his barn. People from miles away would come to take a look at the beast that was caught, until one night it escaped, chains and all. In my opinion, I believe it was also a juvenile Sasquatch. I don't believe an adult would allow themselves to be caught. I also believe due to an adult male's strength and weight it would be quite difficult to catch and carry. The juveniles are still relatively large compared to us, just not as big as the adult males.

The Shadow Man

Another student from the high school began to share her stories of encounters with the "Shadow Man". She described where she lived, and recounted stories of a shadowy figure that lurks in the front yard in the trees. She claims that several neighbors in the area have reported the creepy shadow man. No one has ever caught him, he seems to be around when she is alone and there are few witnesses. He stands maybe eight to ten feet tall according to the witnesses. He doesn't run and hide, he just stands there lurking in the shadows and stares. They can't make out features or a face, just the black mass in the shadows of the trees. I took her story and account and documented what she told me. I also noted her physiological responses to stress and fear. I have also known this student for three years. She is a first generation immigrant. English is her second language. Even though she wanted to believe in Bigfoot, I believe her culture, her native beliefs and folklore would not allow her to accept that this creature could possibly be the same creature I was witnessing on the ranch. She never once described it as an animal, it was a man. She was adamant that it was evil and dark in nature, spiritual and haunting. It was easier and much more acceptable for her and her family and community to believe in the magical and mystical aspects of this being, than to believe in the flesh and blood wood ape creatures that so many are claiming and trying to convince us that exists in the woods today.

I accepted her account and believed 100% of everything she had reported. I did not dare judge her. I understood everything she told me. I also believed that her "Shadow Man", and the ten footer the teenage hunter had seen were one in the same. It turns out the location where he had been hunting and had his sighting, and where she and her family lived, were the exact same location. This is an example of how two different individuals with different backgrounds and different cultures as well as levels of knowledge and understanding and beliefs can honestly describe and experience the same exact phenomena, but choose to call it by a different name.

I could go on and on. Since publishing this book, I have heard more stories of sightings and experiences in my area. I believe more people are aware of these creatures than we realize. I also believe our area has a deep history of these people. It didn't take long before I began to receive personal accounts from adults.

The Neighbor

One day as I waited at the cattle guard to pick up the boys as they were dropped off by the school bus, I noticed a blue truck at my neighbor's house. He sped towards me and kicked dust and gravel in his path. I was scared. What could he possibly want? I did not know this guy. He was a big burly guy with gages in his ears. He had salt and pepper hair and a salt and pepper beard. He began to scold me and asked me if I owned a small black and brown dog. I said I did. That was Wendy he was talking about. Then he mentioned that she had been going around to neighbors' houses and eating the cat food and harassing the animals. He warned me that I ought to tie up my dog before people start taking matters into their own hands. He said she had been chasing my neighbor's chickens. My neighbor was away on vacation and this gentleman was keeping an eye out on his property. I was kind of nervous and tried not to show my fear and explained to the nice man that I couldn't and wouldn't tie up my dog. I needed her to protect our property and my kids from all the creatures that are lurking around our house. Now I could list quite a few. I wasn't necessarily referring to the Sasquatches. Then he shot me that look. That look I had seen before. He then began to mention that he was having some strange activity at his house down the road. Then I studied his face and wondered if I should tell him "my" truth. Then I told him that I knew what it was that was lurking around his house at night and scaring his animals. Then he sighed and ran his big burly hands over his beard and he took a deep breath. I then asked him if he would like me to tell him what was lurking around his house at night and bothering his animals. I waited for the go ahead, and I got it. I said, "It is Bigfoot."

The look on his face was priceless. His eyes got bigger and he leaned forward and said, "I KNEW IT! I KNEW IT!" "Gosh Darn It I Knew It!" He then began to describe what he had seen recently. He had heard all the commotion outside and as he tried to look out of his bay window, a creature was standing there, possibly four feet wide and taller than the windows and the eaves of his house. I told him that was the Big Daddy. He said," most people won't acknowledge what they have seen, for fear people will think they are crazy, but when you talk about it, well, it makes sense and you put in words that don't make it seem crazy". Wow! I was so surprised by his response. I quickly drove back to the house to get him a book. I was also relieved, because Wendy was off the hook!

The Hairy People In The Woods

One story I had heard was from a colleague of mine. She claims she was raised thirty miles away from where I live. She also claims that the people during that era knew all about the people in the woods. She said it wasn't strange. There were a lot of people who chose to shun society and live among themselves in the woods. Yes, they were much more primitive and kept to themselves, and that is how they viewed them. She claims her cousin had an encounter with the Hairy People In The Woods. She even called the police and her story was written up in the local newspapers. She claims she was sitting in a rocking chair out on her porch when a tall hairy person came right up to her porch and startled her. She stated that in those days it was just common knowledge. No one ever called them Bigfoot. Later on in the year I plan to interview her cousin and take a tour of the area. I would like to document and research this story.

The Bigfoot Village

Another colleague of mine told me an even more fascinating story that has left me speechless. I plan to help her write her own book, since I think it needs to be told. She had heard of my book but she had not made the connection, until one day I had to tell her what had happened to us on January the 2nd of 2014 that nearly caused us to move. I don't know why I chose to tell her of all people. I didn't tell anyone. She looked at me and began to share her experiences. She didn't refer to the Sasquatches as people, she referred to them as entities. She then proceeded to describe the ranch where she grew up, which is also thirty miles away from our ranch. She claims they had pecan groves. She said these entities lived there in the trees. She described the relationship they had with these entities, and how her father decided to build tree houses in the pecan trees. She described multiple tree houses with walkways and bridges in between.

I know what you are thinking, because I did not believe it either. That is until she showed me the pictures. I almost threw up. It was that same feeling I had in the first book when I found that first set of footprints out by the pond. This turned my world upside down. Till this day I am still trying to process this information. This has taken me into a direction I was not planning on going. She has pictures of these entities in the tree houses, and I can clearly see the railings and the walkway. Then there is a picture of a huge creature. I have to be honest with you I have to squint because these pictures are from her childhood. This woman is now in her late fifties. So these pictures have to be at least forty years old. One picture took my breath away. I have heard a lot of talk about portals and entities and energies and I don't know what to say. My brain is trying to catch up with my heart. It takes a long time for information to make its way from your heart to your head, or your head to your heart.

In other words, I instinctively know what they are since my heart is telling me what they are. I already know. But my brain is taking longer to process this information. So, what did I see that almost made my knees buckle again? I saw a picture of a rather large creature between the trees. There was a light that radiated from behind him and was as bright as the sun. Yet, the light did not come from above the trees, it came from the base of a tree. I was told it was a portal. I cannot ignore this information. I plan to help this woman in any way I can to get her story told, by her and for her, not for me. I just think we all need to know, and would be very blessed to hear her story.

This was the first time I had personally encountered someone with this kind of story. It takes my breath away just thinking and wondering and imagining all the possibilities. I don't know everything. I don't have all the answers. So, I have to take her eyewitness testimony and treat it the same as the others. I believe her. I can't wait to

sit with her and hear more of her stories and her
experiences with the Sasquatch people.

Chapter Nine
The Second Fire

I had finally decided to do some yard work. The weather was perfect! We were having a new satellite dish service installed and I decided we should all be outside in order to let the technician hook up the equipment inside without us getting in his way. I began to cut the hedges in the front of the house. They were so overgrown and really needed to be tended to. I had wanted to replace window screens, since the cats had tried to break their way into the house the first year and a half, but I could not reach the screens since the hedges were so wide and overgrown. So, this was the day I was finally going to cut the hedges. It was a lot of work. The hedges were so thick I had to saw branches off. As I was sawing and clearing branches I found something in the hedges I had not seen in a year and a half. I had found a solar light that I had bought the previous year.

One summer day in 2012 I had gone to the local hardware store and they had these gorgeous pink solar lights. They were round and had cracked glass. They were gorgeous. I bought two since they were so expensive and placed them in the front yard on either side of the sidewalk about twenty feet from the entrance. It made the front yard look so beautiful and gave the front doorway a sort of grand entrance appeal. I bought twenty black solar lights for the backyard and the flower beds around the bird baths. These were much cheaper, so I could afford more. I had noticed within weeks that the cheaper solar lights were disappearing. I just blamed the dogs. I figured they were pulling them out and taking them out into the pasture and burying them. Then the expensive lights disappeared one by one. I figured the cows had gotten into the yard and damaged them and my husband threw them away as he was cleaning the yard. I just assumed he forgot to tell me. So, I never questioned anyone, I just accepted that all the solar lights disappeared over a relatively short period of time.

While I was trimming the hedges that day, things started to add up. I began to clear debris and leaves from under the hedges. I was surprised to find one of my pink solar lights under the hedges. It was broken in half. The glass globe was also broken in half. There is no way they just ended up under the hedges on their own, they were very heavy and the glass was thick and hard to break. I believe someone did not like the solar lights in the yard. I also believe this light had been thrown against the house and intentionally discarded behind the hedges. These hedges were just too thick and overgrown and the solar lights were just too heavy to have been placed behind the hedges close to the brick wall by the dogs or the cats. I stood there in disbelief, and like every other experience we have had on the ranch in the last two years, I began to process what was happening and putting two and two together. I realized right then and there that the dogs had not carried the twenty smaller solar lights off into the pasture and buried them. I then began to wonder if the Bigfoot/Sasquatches had taken these lights for their own use. Now that makes total sense!! Doesn't it? But, the pink globes were totally destroyed, they just didn't take those, they destroyed them. So, was there a problem with lights?

Then I began to wonder if they didn't like all the extra lights on at night.

So, after this discovery I was not sure if I should put Christmas lights up this season. We did not do it last year or the year before. I should have gone with my instinct. I should have left the lights alone. Something kept nagging at me and telling me not to put up lights. There was a reason the other lights were either destroyed or gone.

We finished trimming the hedges and raking the leaves. We carried the leftover debris to the burn pile in the pasture. As we did this I realized it had been almost two years since we had our first fire. I then began to wonder why I had never had another fire out in the pasture again. Then I realized that all of that activity we had experienced during and after the first fire was just too overwhelming. I began to recount the events of the first fire. I remember details that I unintentionally left out of the first book. I think it was because I was still processing the experience.

I wrote about the fire in the first book, and how we had cut tree limbs and saplings from all over the ranch. It didn't help much, because everything grew back within six months. We drug all the branches and debris to the burn pit. We stacked it and started the fire at nine that Saturday morning. As the day went on, we did hear bird calls. We still had not suspected anything. The boys were having a blast. I remember Kirk was climbing the tree above me, hanging from the vines. These vines were so huge. I was sawing and removing the new growth around the base of the trees. Kirk lost his grip and fell straight down, head first. Luckily his foot was caught in between two vines. He was securely being held upside down, and not a scratch on him. I remember I was in total shock since it almost seemed as though he was being suspended in midair, upside down. If I didn't know any better, I would have thought that invisible hands were holding my son by his ankles.

Later that night as it became darker, the boys decided to go inside and take their baths. Daphene and I stayed outside by the fire sitting in our lawn chairs. It was around nine. By then we were well aware that around that time you could see satellites overhead in the night sky. We were also able to see the international space station, which we thought was so cool. The next thing we heard while gazing into the night sky was a loud thud. We knew something huge had just jumped out of a tree near us. We just looked at each other and decided it was time to head inside. We then put out the fire with the buckets of water. The next day Daphene found all the buckets in the fire pit with only one side melted. So, that was the first fire. We had not had another fire in twenty months. As I claimed in a previous chapter, I can predict their behavior. There was so much activity surrounding the first fire experience, I avoided having another fire for almost two years. That is how sure I was. I instinctively knew that having a fire would guarantee activity and possibly an encounter. I really did not need a Philosophical Mathematical Theory such as Salmonoff's Theory to figure out that one plus one equals two. It was purely due to common sense. Remember all the research I had done but decided to get rid of? Well, this was one of the items I researched.

For those people who do not believe in the existence of Bigfoot/Sasquatch because they believe there is no probative, scientifically verifiable evidence that Bigfoot exists, I offer Salmonoff's Theory. Which in laymen's terms means, if I can mathematically predict outcomes, behaviors, and responses that in itself is verifiable scientific evidence.

Why do you think all those wood ape chaser are dressing up in camouflage on weekends and heading for the woods with sound equipment and night vision cameras in very specific locations? They are predicting outcomes based on previous data. There! That is all I'm giving you!

In conclusion, the reason I did not want to have another fire is because I was 100 percent positive that we would have activity. The link and the attraction and the reason for the behavior was due to the fire, and I will go one step further, it was due to their fascination with fire.

I could not put it off any longer. It was time, since we could not pile up any more tree branches and debris. They had to be burned. So, this was the weekend. The satellite installer finished his job and then asked us if we would like to have him discard the old dish for us. Oh we laughed so hard at that one. He probably thought we were crazy. Remember the satellite graveyard? We got rid of that the first year. Now this guy is asking what to do with the old dish. So, I had to tell him our Bigfoot story. I also gave him a book and signed it. He was very nice and very grateful and then left, and took the old satellite dishes that were on the roof with him.

When I was done cutting the hedges I began to put Christmas lights on the roof. I was not sure if this was a good idea, since there had already been too much going on for one day. I decided to put up only one set of lights. I wanted to see if they would enjoy the lights or not. After finding the broken solar light in the hedges, I knew I was asking for trouble. I went ahead and used only one box. It was getting late and we all came inside and got ready for bed. It was maybe 8:00 p.m. and really dark outside and the dogs were having a fit. I had never heard so much barking. It was scary. There was obviously something outside that the dogs did not like. We brought them inside and put them in their cages, and they continued to bark. I knew I was not going to be able to put up Christmas lights. There was no point. Two days later all the lights were on the ground. Oh well, I tried!

By now you know me. I just do not let things sit. I started researching Bigfoot and Christmas Lights. There is a book on Kindle called "Bigfoot and the Wooden Cross and Christmas Lights." These people have a story to tell about Bigfoot visiting when they put their lights up. Unfortunately, we were not so lucky. We were not allowed to put up Christmas lights or have solar lights outside. Someone does not want any lights outside at all. I thought that was strange since the houses along the highway are all decorated with lights. Then I wondered if they were just too far out in the open and too visible to the public for the Squatches to mess with. Then I just decided that they did not want anyone to see us at all, any of us. You cannot see my house from the highway. There are just too many trees. So many locals have commented on how they always wondered what was back there behind the trees in the woods. They had heard about the two story house and the hundred acre ranch with the two ponds and the lake and two huge barns deep in the woods, but they had never seen them. I think the Bigfoot/Sasquatches wanted to keep it that way. And as I mentioned before, I was letting them take the lead, after all it was there place, not ours.

So back to the fire, it was too late to start a fire on that Saturday after the hedges were done. We had to wait till Sunday morning. My husband woke up early and headed outside to get it all started. The year before I was so eager and gung-ho to get it started. This year I stayed in the house. I really had to do some self-reflection and realized I was really afraid to go out to the pit. I knew the fire the year before had attracted them, and I really did not want a face to face encounter like the one my husband had. So, I waited till four o'clock p.m. then I went to check on my husband and the boys, who were tending the fire. Well, my husband was tending the fire. My boys were roasting marshmallows and hot dogs using these long skewers we had found in the camping section at the local Walmart. Yup, no more wire hangers for us. They were just perfect.

My husband was no longer a skeptic. He could see everything clearly. He looked at me and asked if I would stay and watch the fire while he went to town and picked some stuff up at the store. I said okay. Before I could sit in the lawn chair he motioned to the tree behind him and said, "Keep your eye on that tree." "I saw a little one scurry up the tree when we came out this morning." "Tomorrow look for footprints." I said, "Gee thanks." Then he left.

Yup he left me there all alone with a Squatch in a tree watching me tend the fire. I kept looking up at the tree and could not help but laugh. I knew it was a baby. Oh My God! A little kid cannot stand still for thirty seconds let alone six hours. The leaves were still green and had not turned and fallen yet. So, I could not see anything in the trees. He was well hidden. I could see however, every fifteen minutes or so, fifty leaves or more showering to the ground every time it moved. I could not help it, I broke out in my best Madea accent and told him, "to get down off that tree and come and join me here by the fire." Then I broke into my best Eddie Murphy accent from Nutty Professor, and continued with, "come on Cletus, get yourself down here and sit right here!" "Come on Cletus!" "Come on!" "We all know you're there." "You know I am here." "So, come on now!" Not bad for a white girl. I was just in the mood. I could never be a Bigfoot Hunter or Squatcher. I am just too loud, flamboyant, and silly. I cannot take anything seriously, not even this. I mean really, who are we kidding? Enough already! Just get off the damn tree and show yourself. What ya waitin for? Then it got even better.

I pulled out my new drum. I had found it at St. David's Thrift store in Dallas on Northwest Highway right next to Bachman Lake. I remember leaving the store and a gentleman stopped me when he saw my drum. He knew I had just made the biggest find of the day. These things are priceless. I bought it for five bucks. It was a real custom made Native American drum, not manufactured. I could spot a fake, after all, I had lived in Taos New Mexico. People always try to fake real Native American products.

So, I sat there tending the fire, sitting in the lawn chair and began to pound out the beat to a little ditty I remember from my campfire days. The Wo He Lo Song. I pounded so loud and sang the words I can still remember after *# years. (That was not a typo, I am just not telling you how old I am. Besides a girl's gotta keep some secrets, although I do have more than most!) So, as I said in the first book. I do not plan to live in fear. So, I might as well have some fun with them while I am here. Right?! Okay, I realize I am contradicting myself here. At first I did not want to come outside because I was really afraid. But then, when I was left in the situation, humor took over. That is apparently how I handle my fear. I turn to comedy. I know it is weird, but it works for me. I continued drumming and singing a few more songs from my youth.

My husband came home and took over the fire duties and I went inside to get myself ready for bed. The next day was a school day. That evening I asked my husband if he had put out the fire. He too used the same method as I did and had buckets filled with water at the ready. When I asked if he had left the buckets out he looked at me in disbelief, "Of course not!" he replied. "I put everything in the garage!" "Okay, I was just checking."

The very next day we sent the kids to school and my husband, the reformed skeptic, called in to work and took a personal day off. He headed out to the burn pit. He took the day off! He never does that. He was that confident we would find something. I quickly joined him. He pointed out that he had left out the wire skewers the boys used to roast marshmallows and hotdogs. He could not see them in the dark the night before, so he failed to put them away.

Imagine if you were a Baby Squatch sitting in a tree watching these skinny hairless creatures around a fire with these wire sticks in their hands topped off with a white spongy bulb at the end. What would you think? What would you do? Well, monkey see, monkey do, just like the year before. My husband said the first thing he noticed when he reached the fire was a wire skewer sticking straight out of the cold coals. God I thought that was adorable!

Then we headed towards the tree. It turned out to be three huge oak trees all about five to seven feet apart. So, from our vantage point it looked like one huge oak tree. It also explained how "he/she" could remain unseen. There were a lot of places to hide. We then surveyed the ground around the tree and found what we were looking for, and this time I took a picture. We found the most perfect footprint in the sand. It measured about eight to nine inches long and four to five inches wide. It was clearly barefooted and heavy and headed in the direction of the fire pit. My husband then noticed another footprint in the clay soil closer to the fire pit. This footprint was harder to see since that soil is much more solid. I can make out the heal print and the toes. I placed a stick right next to it to give you an idea of the length of the print. This was clearly a baby. I guess his parents trust him with us or us with him. Who knows, they might have been within earshot. I was totally aware of this possibility.

Figure 5 Baby Sasquatch footprint in sand found Nov. of 2013.

Figure 6 Baby Sasquatch footprint found on hard clay in Nov. of 2013.

Okay, here is my humble opinion based on my observations, eyewitness accounts, and good old fashioned common sense, after all, I am the one on the front lines here. This was truly a baby. A large creature could not "scurry" as my husband described. The Juvy Squatch from the year before was built like a six foot prepubescent teenager. So I am guessing his prints would have measured in the twelve inch range or more. This baby's prints were clearly eight to nine inches in length, much smaller. I am thrilled to know there is a baby out there watching me. It has relieved some of the anxiety I had before. It was really unsettling imagining a ten foot creature watching me daily. I can handle knowing a curious baby is hanging in the trees just watching me as I go about my daily life. I also believe this could be the one waiting in the brush by the cattle guard just waiting for my boys to get off the bus every day. It all makes so much sense.

It took my husband two to three days to come down from that experience. By then he was able to give me more details of the night of the fire. He said that around nine o'clock, he saw the shadow come down from the oak tree. He just knew it must have been a baby. It walked in the shadows maybe 15 to 20 feet behind them. It went from tree to tree and then "snuck" up to the barn just behind them. I say it "snuck" up since I believe it assumed it was in stealth mode and invisible, but my husband could clearly see it lurking in the shadows. Then as my husband and youngest son were glaring at the fire they noticed five shadows. They could account for the two of theirs, and my husband knew there was a baby just behind him, but they had no idea about the other two shadows that were cast upon the fire. It was at that moment my youngest decided he was done and had to come inside. So my husband had to quickly put out the fire, collect the buckets, and bring him inside.

There it is, predictable behavior, visual sightings, multiple witnesses, and footprints. What else do you need? This all happened within 20 yards from the house.

Chapter Ten
To Give or Not To Give
That Is The Question

So, after the fire I began to really think about that baby and I started to feel really bad. I then wondered if he or she was the one who was so interested in my boys the first year. Could this little creature be the one who knocks on their windows and calls their names and visits their dreams? Could this be the tender, loving little soul who gave my boys the gifts more than twenty two months ago? I have thought about those gifts for twenty two months. I have often thought about who it was that decided to give my sons toys, more specifically, a basketball, and a soccer

ball. In the first book I told you that my husband had
thrown them out since the dogs had never touched them let
alone played with them, which I found unusual. We had a
dog at the time who tore up any ball the boys left outside,
that is any ball, but these given by the Sasquatches. I hate
to admit it but we were just so freaked out by the gestures.
We didn't know what to do with them. We were still in
shock. We were still trying to process the fact that we had
Sasquatches coming to our house and knocking on our
windows and walls. So, we did not know how to respond to
the gifts, and therefore chose not to play with them. We
just put them on the central heating unit outside and just
glanced at them every time we walked by them on our way
out the back door. One day they were gone so I assumed
that whoever gave us the gifts had taken them back, or my
husband had thrown them away while cleaning the yard.

The weekend of the fire when I had decided to put
up Christmas lights, (which was a huge mistake) I was
surprised to find the small soccer ball that had been gifted
to my boys almost two years before. While I was looking for
the extension cords in the garage I was rummaging through
their plastic toy bins. I was shocked to see the small round

and dirty soccer ball among my sons' toys. I grabbed that ball as if it was made of gold. I wrapped it in a plastic bag and placed it in a cooler and placed it high upon a shelf. I was stunned. I could not believe we still had the soccer ball. I did not know where the basketball was, but at least I had found the soccer ball. This was the only proof I had of the gifts that showed up that winter day in 2012, just three months after we had moved to the ranch. After cleaning up the garage and taking debris to the fire pit I finally took hold of my most prized possession. I took it down from the shelf, opened the cooler and unwrapped it from the plastic bag. You would have thought I was handling *Waterford Crystal*. I handled it with kid gloves. I gently held it in my hands and began to rotate it as though I was a diamond jeweller observing every flaw, every crack, every nook and cranny. I was now ready to take it all in. I felt a surge of sadness well up from deep inside my soul and I began to cry. I was ready to face my reality and the truth that lay before me. As I stood there holding this precious little crusty old soccer ball in my hands, I knew I was standing at the forefront of humanity, I was at a *critical point*.

critical point

noun   (Concise Encyclopedia)
In science, the set of conditions under which a liquid and its vapor become identical

I knew I was standing in the doorway between two species. I knew at the very moment that this was the place and time when I realized our two species had united, had communicated, had crossed barriers and bridged the gap. Could this be what unites us? Are we also at the "critical point" when two species begin to realize they are one in the same?

I knew it was time to respond with some kind or form of communication. They had reached out to us two years ago in an attempt to communicate with my boys, and I, out of fear and ignorance had yet to respond. Honestly I had been obsessing over this for almost two years. I have been stuck dead in my tracks unable to respond. Not because I did not think anyone would believe me, but because I knew for a fact that we were experiencing something undeniably profound, and I was afraid.

Figure 7 The first gift, the first year.

So, it has bothered me and stayed with me all this time. The idea that I had never returned the gesture, to the one who gave my boys their balls, has left me feeling utterly and totally guilty. This whole experience has taught me humility, patience and meekness. I feel as though I am the lesser of the two species. I am the one who has to be taught. I am the one who has to be educated and made aware of their presence. I am the one who is slowly discovering this new yet ancient reality. I am the one searching for understanding. They are the teachers. They are the ones allowing me to know and experience them. I have been completely humiliated beyond understanding. I cower at my knees when I realize no amount of education, intelligence, or arrogance could have prepared me for life here on the ranch. That is what holding this ball, this precious gift, in the palm of my hands does to me. It brings me to my knees and makes me realize, we have it all wrong.

I knew I was scared and trying desperately to understand and process this stuff, learning and discovering everything I could about them and coming to the realization that we have these amazing creatures in our presence and on the ranch. But, there was no excuse for not giving a gift back, especially when I realized the gifts must have come from the Baby Squatch. After the fire, and after realizing there was a much smaller creature on the ranch, possibly the same age as my youngest son, I really began to feel guilty. It was at that same exact time that I found the soccer ball in the garage. So, seeing the soccer ball made me realize how big of a deal all of this really was. It also made me realize how extremely brave he or she was to make that kind of contact. This baby, this child had no fear. He or she was willing to break convention, risk the dangers associated with making contact in order to give my sons a gift. My heart breaks to think that Baby had been waiting for twenty two months for a response. At this moment I began to realize and accept that these creatures were in no way animals. I knew for a fact at that moment, just standing there looking at that soccer ball, that I was dealing with sentient beings capable of intentional meaningful communication. These were no animals, these were not apes. I was able to truly understand and see them for who they truly are. They are people just like us.

Now I have heard of Bigfoot "experts" who received their cryptozoology degrees and certifications from a Cracker Jack box proclaim that this gifting is equivalent to and similar to how animals give gifts. Yes, I agree, my dog could have gone out there and dug up two small eight inch balls and placed them exactly and perfectly next to the basketball goal on the driveway equal distances apart. Had it been the dogs retrieving these gifts from a neighbor's ranch, then I would have continued to receive gifts. My dogs would have continued to raid the neighboring ranches for two years and random toys would have been strewn across my yard. That did not happen. Since I am the observer, I am the witness, I am the one experiencing and analyzing every aspect of this ongoing activity, I am the one who is going to make the declaration and proclamations here. These toys were not gifted by animals. These toys were intentionally gifted by a very young Sasquatch.

Chapter Eleven

The Gifting Tree

The last week in November I had made the decision to begin a gifting program. I know that sounds so formal, but it had to be well thought out, consistent and intentional. After all, I believe the Baby Squatch had put an awful lot of thought and effort into our gift. I first carefully sought out a location to begin our exchanges and decided on the perfect spot. I picked a huge oak tree out in the pasture between the pond and the lake. This was no ordinary tree. It had been struck by lightning the year before and had been split into many pieces. I picked this tree since it was between the house and the woods, relatively close to cover, so they would not have to remain in the open too long.

This is the gifting tree on a cold foggy morning. I took this picture from a different angle facing towards the lake and swamp.

Figure 8 The gifting tree on The Bigfoot Ranch.

Here is a picture of the same gifting tree from a different angle. I took this picture with my back towards the lake and facing towards the house. Notice you cannot see the house at all. This location gives them ample coverage. All the fallen tree limbs also keeps the cattle and the longhorns away from the gifts. This picture was taken in the dead of winter.

Figure 9 Same gifting tree facing west.

I placed a basket of golden delicious apples approximately four feet up in the tree. I placed it there so they could clearly see the basket since there were no leaves to cover the gifts. I also placed it there so the wild hogs could not reach the basket, it was up off the ground, yet within reach. I intentionally placed the basket there facing the woods so they could see it as they came into the clearing just beyond the woods. This tree was in a very secluded area of the ranch, we are the only people who would be able to see the tree. I have to take a bit of a hike just to check on the basket, or drive my van to the tree.

Here is a view of the ranch from my side of the house. Even standing outside in the backyard, you can't see the gifting tree. I added several other pictures of the ranch so you can truly see what I see. Looks like heaven to me.

Figure 10 Looking towards the gifting tree from the backyard.

Figure 11 View of the lake from my bedroom window.

I absolutely love this picture. This is the view of the lake that I wake up to every morning. All I have to do is look right outside my bedroom window downstairs. The kids have a better view from the second floor.

Figure 12 This is the picture of the basket in the gifting tree.

This is the picture of the basket in the tree. I did not take a picture of the basket of apples. Why? I don't know. I am just learning as I go. Like I have said before, I am not an expert, I am not a researcher, and I am not a Bigfooter or Squatcher. I did not think about taking pictures of the basket filled with apples. I finally did take a picture of the same gifting basket with the shell box and Christmas ornament several weeks later.

Chapter Twelve

Apples and Oranges

Why now? I am ready! You are ready! We are all ready! We all want to know everything about them. How intelligent are they? Do they think like us? Who are they? Where do they come from? Do you realize we know nothing about them? I don't know what to tell you, but this year it just felt right. I also felt so much support from my family, friends, colleagues, and readers around the world. I was no longer afraid. I felt like Dian Fossey. I was ready to initiate contact after almost two years of waiting. Speaking of Dian Fossey, I think another reason I was so obsessed with the gifts was because I was still trying to interpret and

intellectualize the whole situation. I was trying so hard to
understand what they were trying to communicate by giving
us these gifts. I was thinking of Dian Fossey and Jane
Goodall during this time. We knew virtually nothing about
primates and the great apes. Dian spent time with the great
apes in the Congo, and learned about their family dynamics,
mannerisms, and habits. She is greatly credited for helping
humanity understand the great apes. Jane Goodall is known
for her research on the chimpanzees. I met her when she
came to speak at my college in the late eighties. So, I know
their work well, and I had no idea how important all that
information that was stored in my brain would be twenty
years later. So, with all of this information we have on other
primate species we can make certain assumptions,
especially since many of the same traits that the great apes
possess, we possess as well. So even though we know very
little about Sasquatch/Bigfoot we can make certain
assumptions. One assumption I made, based on primate
behavior and human behavior is that we are all territorial
and we protect our young. That is one of the reasons I
maintained my distance and continued to remain cautious.

I had heard someone say on a podcast interview,

"We cannot impose our expectations, our thoughts, our morals, and our values on these creatures. They are not like us." I believe this fool was an anthropologist. Yes, that is what has gotten us into global conflicts around the world, since we continue to see ourselves as "others", and not having a thing in common. This isolationist attitude keeps people separated and in constant conflict and turmoil, yet we continue to celebrate our "otherness", or specialness, which I believe is our arrogant insatiable need to maintain our superiority by declaring members of the same species as inferior to us.

There are those in the Bigfoot Community who now have decided to put forth the idea that Sasquatch/Bigfoot is a "lower" primate and just a big dumb ape living in the woods, needing to be hunted down, and dissected and analyzed like some lab rat. I was almost convinced (for about five hundredths of a second) and then I decided that maybe the real intent and actual hidden agenda of some of these Bigfoot groups in changing this one little detail would allow ignorant, uneducated, arrogant human beings to accept the possibility of the existence of Sasquatch/Bigfoot if we think they are not like us. Not human. If we assume they are less than us, members of the lower primates, an undiscovered ape who has gone unnoticed, then it makes chasing, stalking, hunting them down and killing them acceptable to the ape chasers. That makes total sense, if that is your agenda. Declaring them to be animals makes killing them okay and therefore acceptable to those who have a clear agenda. That would make a whole lot of people really comfortable. Hog Freakin Wash!

So where am I going with all of this? Well, this leads me to why I waited twenty two months to respond! I was trying to figure out how to communicate with them, but I was afraid of unintentionally responding and creating a volatile and possibly dangerous relationship that would put my family in danger. I in no way tried to assume they were animals and I absolutely did not want to insult them by treating them as such. I have thought carefully about how to respond, and what to respond with, and what message I was sending. I kept trying to "think" like them. Then it hit me exactly two years to the day, since we moved to the ranch. I was trying to really analyze and interpret the intended meaning of the gift. And, like a bolt of lightning that came from out of the cloudy skies, it hit me. They do think like us. There it is. That is my huge proclamation that I am claiming as my own discovery. I, believe that Sasquatch/Bigfoots, think just as we do. Why else would the Baby Squatch leave a basketball and a soccer ball for a nine year old and a six year old boy? How many people this Christmas season bought a basketball or a soccer ball for their sons, daughters, nephews, and nieces, grandchildren, or bosses kid? It is the most logical of all gifts. It is a no brainer.

It took this Baby Sasquatch exactly ten weeks to get to know us through careful daily observations, to determine what kind of gifts my children would appreciate and it has taken me twenty two months to figure out how to respond. It probably wouldn't shock you to know that my kids played on soccer teams and were on basketball teams in 2012. Someone out there was doing their homework! I am really, really embarrassed. I am ashamed of being an arrogant human being and trying so hard to over think, over analyze, and over interpret everything. It was so simple. I was also arrogant enough to think that I was making contact with them, instead of realizing that they were making contact with us. I had it all backwards. I did not go to their house and establish physical contact, they came to mine. I did not dare leave treats and gifts, they left gifts for us. I was under the false impression that I was in charge and in control of this relationship. It has taken me two years to realize, I was wrong. So, all of this leads me to the basket of apples I had placed in the tree. I decided on a simple edible gift, the apple, so universal. (And ironically Biblical, maybe that is why they didn't eat them.)

A week went by and I went to check on the apples. I was so disappointed at first because they were still in the basket, untouched. I also saw at least ten footprints around the tree, there were various sizes. It was obvious that they were curious. After discussing it with Pat, the librarian at work, we decided that they were just being cautious, just like we had been. I mean after all, it has been two years, and suddenly I choose to give them gifts? I can only imagine how suspicious they were of this change in my behavior.

Another week went by and we experienced a drastic change in temperature. We had gone from 80 degrees during Thanksgiving to 25 degrees just one week later. It also rained so I postponed my trip to the basket until the weather was warmer and the ground was drier. I did not want to get my van stuck in the wet sand out in the pasture.

Finally, on December 11, 2013 the weather was much more agreeable. I was prepared to make the trek out to the basket in the gifting tree. The temperature had finally climbed above 50 degrees that day. I went out to check on the basket and was shocked to see that the apples had remained untouched. I gave up and threw the apples on the ground. I figured at least the wild hogs would eat them, no sense in wasting food. So, I headed back to the house to get ready for work. I remember thinking to myself, "why didn't they like the apples". Then I heard myself contemplating fruit in my thoughts as I drove the twenty minutes to work that day. "You know if I wanted fruit, I would have wanted an orange, you know, maybe I should go to the store after work and buy some oranges." "I love oranges, a nice juicy orange. Okay that settles it. I am getting them oranges." I did not get to the store that day after work, I was waiting for payday and besides it just kept getting colder and colder. I would have to wait a few more days before returning to the gifting tree. A few days later it warmed up and I decided to go check out the basket once again. I found the apples still on the ground. I was totally shocked, and yes disappointed

again, that not even the hogs touched the apples. I was
looking at the apples and noticed a bite mark in one of the
apples. I quickly took my cellphone and took a picture of
what I saw. I also noticed I accidently left the sticker on the
apple. Amateur move! I know, like I said before, I am not
an expert! Say what you will, but those look like dental
impressions to me. They don't look like dog, coyote, wolf,
hog, deer, or horse dental impressions. Even though, a
woman on twitter, the same one as before, had commented
on these impressions possibly having been made by a
coyote. What? Huh? Maybe a coyote with some serious
dentures!

In my opinion, the dental impressions on the apple
looks very similar to ours. This apple looks like a human
could have bitten into this delicious apple. In my humble
opinion, I believe the Baby Sasquatch tried to take a bite out
of this apple. This is a rather small dental impression. Had it
been an adult Sasquatch, I believe the apple would have
been completely devoured in one bite. I also believe this
baby Squatch knew the apples were meant for them. I am
sure I was being carefully observed, as I am every day. It
was the gift the baby had waited for, for almost two whole

years. I also believe that a very cautiously suspicious parent slapped the apple out of his/her mouth and tiny hands and threw it to the ground, admonishing him/her in the process, and warning him/her never to trust the hairless ones. I remember the evening during the summer when I had heard the Mama scolding her young children for coming so close to the house at night. I can hear you now. How and why am I speculating? I have to be honest with you, I am not. When I stepped into the area of the fallen tree, and had seen the apples on the ground and noticed the bite marks, the scenario was already playing in my head. It is as if I was there watching it play out before me as it happened. I assumed I was picking up residual energy and impressions that were left by the Sasquatches, an ability I have had all my life, and an ability that is now stronger than ever before, since we moved to the ranch. I was so sad for the little one, he was never going to enjoy his gift.

Figure 13 Here is the picture of the apple I found on the ground next to the gifting tree.

The next day I was stuck in the kitchen making Christmas cookies for my after school culinary arts class. That morning my husband took the boys to the cattle guard to wait for the bus. This year the bus came at 6:35 a.m. instead of 6:15 as they had done the year before. Thank God! I had just given up last year and started driving the boys to school at 7:20 a.m., which gave me enough time to turn around and go back the twenty five miles to my job in another county. The new later time meant my husband could drive them to the bus stop and see them off. That morning I began to prepare my cookie dough for baking. About fifteen minutes after they had left, which would make it 6:45 a.m. and pitch black outside, I heard a loud noise. I immediately assumed it was a car door slamming, because that is what made sense to me. I assumed it was my husband who had come back to kiss me good bye. Nope! It was not. He has only done that once (Wishful thinking!). I ran to the back door near the laundry room and looked outside expecting to see him, and no such luck. His car was not in the driveway. I rolled my eyes and thought to myself, "just another day on the Bigfoot Ranch." Then I heard the noise on the roof. I rolled my eyes and took a deep breath and said a small prayer and then I tried to put the thought out of my mind. I wanted to leave the ranch, but I could not I had to bake these cookies for class. So, I turned the TV up and played games on the computer while the cookies baked. Anything to avoid the noises I heard outside and on the roof.

That day was early release day and I had planned to meet the boys at the cattle guard so they would not have to walk the half mile down the driveway in the cold. I left the house at 12:45. I arrived at the cattle guard at 12:47. I met the mail carrier who had a package for Kirk, from Grandpa and Grandma, since his birthday was later in the week. The bus came at around 1:15 p.m. and the boys and I headed back home down the long driveway. Once home I continued to bake two more batches of cookies and began to get dressed and ready for work. I was prepared to leave at 2:15 p.m. I carried my cookies and frosting and baking equipment to the back door and headed towards the van. I was shocked and surprised again at what lay before me between my van and the basketball goal that still sat next to the driveway as it had twenty two months before. There on the driveway was an orange. Strange, I know. This time around my brain processed the information much faster. I placed my baking supplies in the van and then I reached for my cellphone and took five pictures. I needed to leave for work so I did not have time to assess the situation. I yelled for Zack and he came outside running, in his underwear! Really, 50 degrees, oh these Texas boys! I made sure he was not in any of the photos. Daphne was off at college, so I needed a new witness, and by default that was Zack. Kirk came outside also. We all observed the orange, and then I laid it next to the basketball goal and headed for work. Halfway down the highway I reached for my cellphone and called my mom in Dallas. I asked her, "Mom, where are the nearest orange groves in Texas?" She said, Victoria. There could possibly be orange groves much closer to the ranch. I immediately told her about the orange, and it made sense. They could easily pick oranges from an orange grove within a hundred mile from the ranch. I hung up and continued on my way to work.

I was at work for a few hours and then my mind started processing the information I had visually and intellectually observed. This is what I saw. The orange was a freshly clean cut orange. It had been cut with something sharp. It was completely cut into two halves, and then partially cut again into quarters. It was cut in such a way that it would have been easy to pull apart. There was precision, purpose, a method, and intent.

Yes, you read that right the orange was cut in half. Yes folks! That means someone is using tools! Not just any tools, precision tools.

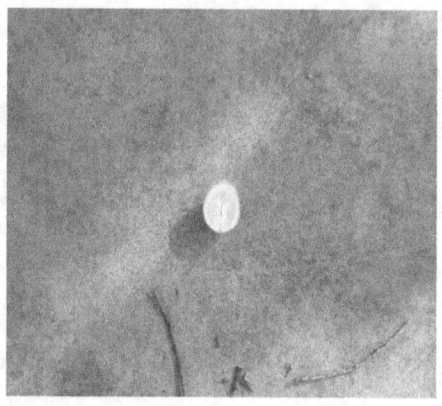

Figure 14 Here is the first picture of the orange I found on my driveway. Found in Nov. of 2013.

This is a picture of the same orange from a different angle. Notice the basketball goal in the background. Also notice no dirt on the driveway, just a few twigs.

Figure 15 Second half of orange I found on the driveway in Nov. of 2013.

This is the picture of the second half of the orange. Notice how much closer it is to the van. Also notice absolutely no dirt. I also notice in this picture it is quite obvious this orange is fresh, still juicy, cut just moments before and ready to eat. In my humble opinion, someone cut this orange just for me, and had expected me to eat it right then and there in the driveway. Why else would you cut an orange in half and give it to someone, if not to eat immediately?

Figure 16 Orange Half I found right next to my van in Nov. 2013.

I cropped and zoomed in on this picture. It is the same one as above. I wanted you to notice how fresh the orange was. I did not manipulate the color. It was that bright and fresh. It is blurry since I had to zoom in. What I wanted you to see, is the slice in the middle of the orange. Notice how it isn't cut all the way through. Who does that? I mean Oh My God!! Not only did I receive a freshly cut orange ready to eat, it is sliced into quarters so that I can peel it apart and separate the quarters and eat the juicy treat without any difficulty whatsoever. I only know of one person who would do this. It would have to be a very loving, kind, generous person who wants only the best for me, and she lives 200 miles away in Dallas, and that is my Mama. She was nowhere near the ranch that day.

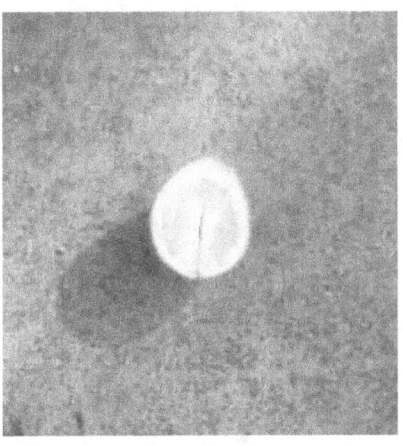

So once I finished work and made the long drive home, I stopped by the basketball goal on the driveway and collected my treat before heading inside. I was so filled with joy and pride. Words really cannot describe how full my heart felt. I immediately went to my office and placed the orange on my desk. I proceeded to take these pictures to show you that there were no puncture marks, since I knew people would question the possibility of whether or not a dog could have brought it to my driveway untouched, fresh, and clean. Also, if a dog had brought it from someone's trash bin or a neighboring ranch, how did he manage to get both halves in his mouth, and without puncture marks? At this point, almost three and a half hours have gone by and the orange is obviously not fresh anymore and has begun to dry out. I felt really bad, since I bet he or she was sitting somewhere close buy just waiting to watch me or my boys devour the juicy orange.

(This picture to me is priceless. You will never understand how I feel each time I see these pictures. I have to catch my breath and let it sink in once again. A Sasquatch gave me an orange as a gift.)

Figure 17 Close up of orange. Notice the slice in the middle.

This next picture is the view of the back of the orange. Once again notice no puncture marks, no claw marks. There are however two very distinct, very precise, and intentional slices. I am just baffled by how precise the cuts were and how sharp the blade must have been. Anybody missing any knives? Anybody out there still think we should be chasing wood apes? Huh, Bueller? Bueller? Anyone? Anyone?

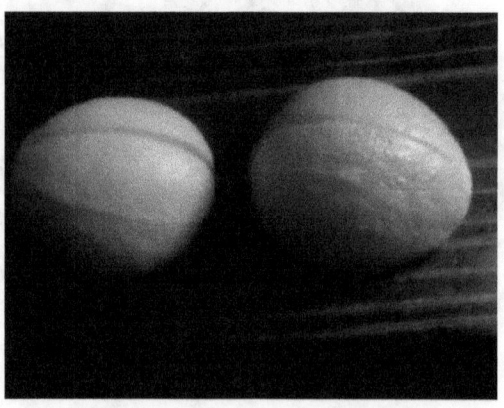

Figure 18 Back of the Orange.

Where did the orange come from? I know, everyone
is thinking I am stupid. The dog is the most logical
explanation. Well, the dog, Wendy (real name, she is not
worried about her identity) was in trouble. Remember the
neighbor who scolded me about her roaming the other
properties? Well, I had to put her in a harness and tie her to
a cable which we attached to a stake. My two sons thought
that was cruel and unusual punishment, so instead I chained
her to a brick. She still had the freedom to roam about the
yard. I could not see her running down the driveway to the
neighbor's ranch and attempt to chase his chickens with a
cement brick at the end of a twenty foot cable. I also could
not see tying her down and not having the ability to get
away from any of the creatures that roamed the ranch. All I
could picture was that scene from Jurassic Park. You know
the one I am talking about, it is the feeding scene. In that
scene they were feeding the Tyrannosaurus and they had
that little goat tied to a stake. Ugh! I just could not do it! I
even let her off leash as soon as I got home. So, there is a
possibility that it could have been Wendy, but I seriously
doubt it. It could not have been Pickles either. She weighed
only eight pounds at the time and her mouth was so tiny she
would have left tiny bite marks on the edges. So, no,

logically and realistically none of our animals delivered this gift.

My mind quietly continued to assess the situation, not like the year before where there was panic and shock and crashing thoughts in my brain. This was different, much more logical, analytical, and calm. I knew who I was dealing with and I began to wonder if this was the response I was expecting for the last two weeks.

Then suddenly all the pieces quietly came together in my brain. "They could have the ability to cut things." "Apes use tools, why wouldn't a Sasquatch?" We know absolutely nothing about them so we are truly unaware of their capabilities. So, at this point and time, everything is a possibility. The next piece of information I was assessing, was that the orange was perfectly fresh and perfectly cut, and perfectly clean. If the dog had dragged it in from another ranch, it would have been dirty and filled with puncture marks. Also, while I was writing this I had a huge epiphany. There were two orange halves. How could any dog carry both halves from a distant ranch? Also, the neighbor south of the ranch moved to town months before due to the "hunting" activity. The neighbor to the north was

away on vacation. So, the closest neighbors were gone.
There was no one to steal food from, and no garbage was
left out. No, in my opinion, these orange halves were gently
and once again intentionally placed on my driveway by a
pair of hands. The orange was perfectly cut and quartered
by a pair of hands. This gift was left within feet of where the
first gifts, the soccer ball and basketball had been
intentionally placed on either side of the basketball goal on
the driveway almost two years ago.

Now let's talk about the timing. The orange halves
were laid right next to my van where I could see them as I
left for work. I consistently leave for work at the same time
every day. They placed the orange on the driveway exactly
between 1:15 p.m. and 2:15 p.m. on a Wednesday
afternoon. There was nothing on the driveway when I
picked up the boys from the bus at the end of the driveway.
We definitely would have seen the orange halves as we
exited the van in the driveway. I am also guessing they
thought I would not be checking the basket due to the cold
weather. So they wanted to make sure I received my gift,
freshly cut and ready to eat! Just saying it (writing it) makes
the hair on my arms stand on end. Do you realize what this

means? Do you realize the intent behind this? I wanted to cry! I was so overwhelmed. This was huge! Then I realized something else. Why did they choose to give me an orange? Had they heard my thoughts? Had they heard me contemplating the kind of fruit I liked and how I had intended to go buy them some oranges the second I got paid? Apparently so. That explains why I had received a freshly cut orange.

Later that night there was more activity around the house. I had decided I would return this gesture much quicker than I had done the last time. So, that weekend I sent the boys out to the tree with an apple fruit bar and a homemade chocolate chip and pecan pancake. Yup, delicious! That is how we like our pancakes. I also picked out a simple gift, since I figured just in case food was not the way to go. My mom had given me this huge box filled with odds and ends for my after school art class. I picked out this box that was covered in seashells and had googley eyes on the top of the box. I also picked out a Christmas ornament that had greenery and gold. I had heard on "Finding Bigfoot", that they liked shiny things. So, I left the ornament in the shell box.

Two nights later I woke up at 1:55 a.m. I awoke just in time to hear a faint roar in the distance. It almost sounded as if someone had found their gifts and was saying "I found them." I documented the time. The next day I drove to the tree and nothing had been touched, by anything, not even coyotes or raccoons. I left it there and checked on it several days later. Still, a week later and nothing had been touched. I know they are only being cautious. I have left the gifts there and check on them from time to time. I am not prepared to take them back. I did come to the profound conclusion that I did not need to select a "gifting" tree somewhere out there. They prefer coming right up to the house. I decided that any other gifts I would give would just be placed on my patio table. I would no longer listen to self-proclaimed experts either. That is where I got the idea of the "gifting tree" and giving a shiny object. For some reason they won't take stuff we try to gift. We eventually realized during the Christmas Holidays that they were taking things from the house, it just took us some time to notice that we had been "giving" each other gifts the whole time.

Chapter Thirteen
Getting Internet Again?

Yes I decided to attempt internet again? I figured if I truly wanted to find out all aspects of this phenomena, I would have to figure out why there had been so much interference with our internet service. I was calling it research. This time I found a local internet provider. I figured it would be much easier to explain it to someone local that something keeps messing with our internet than to call Denver and try to explain it to a complete stranger.

So, Thursday Dec. 19th of 2013 I decided to try internet services again. After delivering Christmas gifts to my boys' teachers I headed twelve miles south to a little store front, off the main highway. They also sell bait, fish, and tackle supplies. "That is so country!" So I arrived and spoke to a sales representative. I started asking twenty questions about service, contracts, fees, and maintenance. Then I asked the big question. "What if I have issues with creatures getting on the roof and messing with our internet or tower?" At first her response was a logical and rational response when I mentioned that the last technician had found that the bolts were being unscrewed from the 10ft radio tower that sits on the second story of our house. She suggested that the screws on the tower had come loose because the installer had possibly used the wrong sized bolts. I seriously doubt that. I do not believe that an installer would be carrying random sized bolts for a standard tower. I believe the equipment is standard and that would be a very hard mistake to make. Hey, my daddy didn't raise a fool! He was a carpenter, craftsmen, rancher, and all around do it yourselfer! So, I was afraid I wouldn't find any answers here. Then, before I could get my next question out, she surprised me. You will not believe what her next response was. She said, "However, we have dealt with issues like that before." "WHAT?!" "REALLY?!" My ears perked up and my eyes widened, and I was waiting to hear more. She said, "We know that there are "monsters" out there messing with our equipment." Can you believe it? I am not the only one! So, I pried and asked for all the details. She said that a customer had a two story house and the cable connecting the radio transmitter on the roof to the computer inside the house had been chewed in half. The cable was up high under the eaves. Impossible for just any animal to reach, they had to be tall and have the ability to stick their head under the eaves and chew the cable. She also said it left huge teeth marks on the house. She said there were pictures, and she showed me the chewed wires and teeth marks. I asked where this happened, and mentioned that I would like to interview these people for this book. The location was within 30 miles of our house.

God! I am starting to feel really normal here. I mean this stuff is just becoming an everyday occurrence. I mean people are starting to speculate about everything that has been going on now. Just last week two very young individuals lost their lives in a car wreck and someone commented to me, "How many times have we wondered why people crash their cars, or spin out and flip with no explanation?" What if there are people out there who are swerving to miss a Bigfoot in the road and end up crashing

and not living to tell about it? It just makes you think.
Wow!

So, back to our new internet service, I had her check
to make sure they covered our area. We were both
surprised when she pulled up the satellite pictures of our
area and showed me where the closest tower to my house is
located. You will never believe it, but the closest tower is at
the end of my driveway near the first cattle guard. Our
neighbors have the main internet tower on their property!
So, we should not have any problems with reception right?
We scheduled the installation for Dec. 23rd of 2013.

I was ready to jump into this aspect of the
Bigfoot/Sasquatch phenomena. I began to research other
reasons our internet could possibly go down without any
logical explanations. Then I began to read some information
on the internet about electromagnetic fields associated with
the Bigfoot phenomena that could possibly cause such
disruptions. This has now led me to research the history of
electromagnetism and electricity in general. I have since
researched Tesla, Clerk, Faraday, Edison, Westinghouse and
various others who were founders in the field. My
conclusion so far is that there are high levels of

electromagnetic energy on the ranch. It comes and goes in waves and cycles. I find it odd that during the two years on the ranch we have lost four large oak trees to lightning strikes. Two were right out in the front yard near the house and two were in the pasture out back. One of them is our gifting tree.

Just recently the house was struck by lightning. I was home and cooking in the kitchen on the electric stove. I heard the strangest noise and saw the large ball of energy. It was a bright glowing orange light that popped right before my eyes. It caused the electric coil on the stove to light up like the sun. It damaged the coil. I was stunned for a few minutes and glad it did not explode in my face. I was even more grateful that the house did not catch on fire. At that moment I became well aware that there was something going on here at the ranch that has to do with very high levels of electromagnetism. This would cause the disruption with the internet, as well as cellphones. I still have horrible cellphone reception despite switching phones and companies. Just the other day as I was working on a few chapters, the electricity went out twice and we completely lost internet service and satellite service. There was no rain storm or lightning in the area. The last time we had a storm roll through a few weeks ago, both towers in the area had been struck by lightning. Both towers are within a mile from the ranch. We had to wait maybe half a day so that both towers could be repaired and service could be restored.

This time we had no service for three days. I tried calling the internet provider's office, but they are closed on weekends, so I had to wait till Monday. When I called, the representative already knew me by name. I thought that was strange since I have only called there twice before. He also called me by my first name. I thought that was really strange. Then I told him we had no service and he began to apologize. He said, "Yes we know the tower at the end of your driveway is down. There has been an inexplicable energy surge and we are investigating it. I will contact you as soon as I know more." Wow, what service. I hadn't even given him my name or my address, and he already knew who I was. See, it is kind of funny because him knowing my name and location before I could even tell him who I was, freaked me out, even more than having a Bigfoot call me by my name. I didn't need to know more, and I wasn't really that concerned. I just thought they needed to know I had no service. I was patiently waiting for internet service to be restored, that is all. I really didn't need an explanation. But, the very next morning the representative from the internet service provider called me back and left a detailed message. He said there had been an inexplicable surge of energy, and it completely fried all of the equipment on the tower at the end of my driveway and every piece had to be replaced. It would take at least a day to repair.

While putting the finishing touches on this book and going over all the "electrical" anomalies occurring on the ranch, I realized something else. Since we have been here on the ranch two plus years, we have also gone through a rather large fairly new television, a lap top with a new battery, that just died, no explanation, and a my trusty old Dell. We took the items to Best Buy and they had no explanation. They just died. Well, they took one look at my old Dell, and immediately called out all the young guys. They wanted them to take a look at the antique computer before it was sent in for recycling. I had to replace all these items. Also, we seem to be replacing light bulbs quite often, especially in my bedroom. I didn't think about it until now, but I wonder if there is a connection with these items? They all require electricity.

What does Bigfoot have to do with any of this? I don't know yet, but that is what I am currently researching. What I can tell you is that adding this element to this phenomena has taken me in a direction I had not expected. I just want you to be reassured, I am not jumping to any conclusions, and I am researching everything before I make any conclusions. What I can tell you at this very moment is that all the wood knocking ape chasers are running in the wrong direction. I honestly think they are actually running around in circles.

It was around this time that I had been told by my friend Mark in Ohio, and by my friend Patricia, that I should be reading Rob Riggs' new book. I have avoided reading other Bigfoot books while I am writing mine. I don't want to confuse experiences or conclusions. I did however take a break and I began to listen to podcasts and interviews with Rob Riggs. I was shocked and amazed. Especially by what Rob had to say about electrical fields, and lights in the night sky that he had witnessed in East Texas. I took a chance and sent him an email. Within 24 hours he responded. He had seen my book and knew who I was. He offered to drop by the area and have a sit down and compare notes. I was absolutely honored to meet him and to have a chance to discuss our very similar backgrounds, experiences and perspectives.

I am getting ahead of myself here, since this all happened well within the third year. I did however want to give you a glimpse of where I was headed. But first, I must finish the second year.

Susan Sullivan

Chapter Fourteen
Christmas Holidays

This whole chapter is basically a repeat of the Short Stories Book, Memories. I am adding this section for individuals who have not read that book. If you have read the book, I am truly grateful. Please forgive me for the repeat. I feel I have to add this section to complete the book. It closes out the whole year and just makes sense. I also published the Memories book since readers were demanding more. So, I put that book together and presented it in a short story format, to keep the reader informed and engaged while I began the Second Year Book.

We sat down to Christmas Dinner this last December the 25th of 2013. Yes, just a few months ago. I made turkey with sausage stuffing, gravy, green beans steamed in butter and bacon, and creamy mashed potatoes. Perfect for a traditional Christmas turkey dinner! I looked around the table at my family. The only one missing was Daphne. She is still in Dallas, enjoying her Christmas Eve birthday and the holidays with new friends. Lucky Daphne, she gets to have a life away from the ranch. Are you surprised that she never wanted to come back? I mean after all she is a teenager and in college. I can only assume she wanted a life that did not involve this daily drama. Besides, teenage girls are notorious for creating their own drama. I have often wondered what the Bigfoot/Sasquatches think about that. I am sure they don't just send their children out into the cold cruel world on their own. I wonder what they think about Daphne being gone, and for so long, and I wonder what they think about us as parents?

While I was fixing dinner, I began to reminisce about everything that had happened since we moved here to the ranch, which I now refer to as the "Bigfoot Ranch in Texas". I was so happy and pleased that we were all in one piece, safe and sound and actually content. We had so much to be grateful for. We have continued to stay here on the ranch despite all of our experiences, and have just learned to accept the weekly activities perpetuated by our noisy and nosey neighbors and their adorable kids. A huge swell of emotion arose deep within me as I realized that we have lived on the ranch for two years. We now have two years' worth of experiences on the ranch in which to contemplate, analyze, mull over, talk about, and write about, you name it. Basically it is two years' worth of data, and evidence that I can now sit and piece together and make serious observations and come up with some serious conclusions. Had we only stayed the first six months like the other renters, we would have been left with such a negative perception of our experiences and many unanswered questions. Now with two years under our belts, we could truly appreciate what was actually going on here on the ranch. I have just learned to turn off the television the second I hear someone debating the existence of Bigfoot/Sasquatch. (Chuckling here, I just heard two distinct knocks while writing that last line. I heard two about three hours ago. I did not dare go outside to check on the noise. Are you kidding, it is 17 degrees outside! I wonder if they know I am writing this right now, and interjected their knocks just at the right time. My they have great timing, and such a sense of humor.)

Back to Christmas dinner. As I was planning, and preparing the meal, Dad had been in the garage putting together game tables, a ping pong table, and an air hockey table just before Christmas dinner. Those were our Christmas gifts to the boys. It was time to get the boys outside again. I could only imagine what the Juvy and Baby Sasquatches will do when they watch us playing ping pong in the garage. I began to chuckle deep inside, wondering if we would suddenly begin to see ping pong balls in the yard in the New Year.

See, a few months ago I had started to notice balls in the yard. I saw tennis balls in the yard next to the garage. We were gone all day, so I figured the dogs were bored and "borrowed" my tennis balls and played with them all day in the yard while we were at work and school. I really did not care. I was glad to know the dogs were playing in the yard while we were gone. The balls, I had assumed, came from my ball hopper in the garage. I was a teacher for the after school program and one of the classes I taught was Tennis.

So, I have this rather large ball hopper that holds maybe eighty balls. The only thing that seemed odd to me was that my balls were fairly new. They had that bright neon greenish yellow color, still fresh out of the can. The balls in the yard were white, dingy, worn, and weathered. I just assumed that they had been bleached by the sun and weathered and aged quickly since they were being played with and left outside daily. I also noticed baseballs in the yard, and I figured they were having a field day with the baseballs as well. We had also coached little league baseball the year before, so having baseballs in the yard would not be unusual. These balls were also worn and weathered, the guts were exposed, and the strings were popped and unraveling. It still did not matter, since we also had a bucket full of baseballs in the garage.

Here is a picture of a tennis ball I found under the hedges amongst the crusty old leaves. Obviously not a new ball, and one I would not be using to play tennis. It is as crusty and old as the soccer ball.

Figure 19 Old tennis ball I found in the yard. Obviously one I would not be using for tennis!

Here is one of the baseballs we found in the yard. We were shocked that we had found several baseballs in this condition.

Figure 20 Baseball I found in the yard this winter.

During Thanksgiving break I had decided to check on the ball hopper in the garage. I thought that the dogs had enough balls to play with, and I was now going to secure the ball hopper so they would not take any more of my new balls. Dad kept throwing the balls in the yard away since they were so old and looked like trash, I was afraid the dogs would continue to dig into my ball hopper for new balls. He just kept cleaning the yard and never questioned anything.

That is why we never have evidence. He throws it away before I realize it is actual evidence. I was shocked when he said he had cleaned up the balls maybe three times, so I was expecting to see a ball hopper with only half the balls remaining or less. The balls in the yard kept appearing, so it only made sense that they were getting them from my ball hopper. So I headed for the garage and I was totally stunned, I mean "just saw a Bigfoot in my backyard" kind of stunned! Not only was the ball hopper closed, and completely secured, it was stuffed with balls. Not one single ball was missing. Now, this is the point when my head starts spinning and my mind starts racing, and I cannot help but say, "What the hell?"

See, it is the little things that we do not notice. That is how they have managed to survive for so long on the periphery of society and civilization. They are so cunning. Okay, so I am not going overboard, after all they are only tennis balls, but I believe this is just the tip of the iceberg.

God I had a great laugh with this one. Ironically, as soon as I discovered that the balls in the yard were not my balls, they stopped appearing. Also, what made this rib tickling knee slapping funny was that my husband and I had discussions about the useless dogs and Wendy's inability to fetch a ball. You can throw a ball at her and she will just sit there and let it hit her, no movement. So, my husband had been discussing getting himself a Golden Retriever for Christmas. I think he might have put it out there that he wanted a new dog. Now that I know a little bit more about all these claims of telepathy among the Bigfoot people I have to wonder if this was a direct response to our conversation. You won't be surprised when I tell you that this conversation occurred inside the house between my husband and myself in our bedroom, no one around but us humans.

When we realized, that these balls were not ours, we could not help but come up with the mental picture of balls being thrown at Wendy from out of nowhere while we were at work, in an attempt to teach her how to fetch. After all, if she did not learn to fetch soon, she was going to be replaced. I know I am truly going out on a limb here, but my conclusion to this experience is based on the fact that it all makes perfect sense. The balls were not all over the yard either. They were in the general vicinity of where the dog lounges. There would be five to ten balls in one spot. So I do have a mental picture of the dog just lying there and balls flying in from out of nowhere and her not moving a muscle. Apparently they could not get her to budge either, and I know they really tried. I am estimating that in total there were maybe thirty tennis balls out on the lawn and ten baseballs.

Okay, I know what you are saying, and I have heard it before. Is it not possible once again, for the dog to have stolen the balls from somewhere and carried them home? Yes, possible, I am all about possibilities, but not likely. I am also all about common sense and telling it like it is. The dogs did not play with the balls. Another question you should be contemplating is, why would she need thirty tennis balls and ten baseballs? One ball would be enough. Did she carry all the tennis balls at once, or did she keep going back time and time again to steal another ball, when there was a ball hopper filled with brand new balls and a bucket of new baseballs in the garage? Hmm, just something to think about...

What is also interesting about all of this, and why these events are so important to point out and notice is because I believe they intentionally picked specific items that were common to us. I coached tennis, so we wouldn't be surprised by tennis balls showing up in the yard. My husband had coached baseball, and we weren't surprised when we saw a baseball in the yard. I started to become alarmed when there were four and five balls in the yard. I was alarmed also by how old they were. I know for a fact I do not hold on to dead tennis balls, you can't use them for tennis, they don't bounce. So I am 100 percent positive those tennis balls in the yard were not mine. The year before, when the boys received a soccer ball and a basketball, they had been on soccer teams that very fall, and were on basketball teams that very spring they received the gifts. Again, if you are not paying attention, these items would be very easy for anyone to overlook. That is why I began to wonder if this year ping pong balls would be showing up. Make sense?

So dad finally decided to take a break from assembling the boys' Christmas gifts. We sat down to dinner and we began to enjoy the feast before us. It had been a memorable year, one we will remember for a long, long time, especially since I have started to document everything.

I began to clean up the kitchen before I sat down for dinner, realizing that I really tried hard to plan this dinner. What I mean is there was not enough room in the refrigerator for more food, so I was carefully planning what to put my leftovers in and how I was going to stack the leftovers and make them fit. Halfway through the dinner Dad had complained that he had nothing to drink. Weird... We have just become so accustomed to not having anything to drink for dinner anymore. Or, should I say not having anything to drink out of anymore. I know we have been busy with work, school, karate, boy scouts, bible study, the Squatches and all the activity that comes with that, but why did we stop having drinks for dinner? That was easy! No cups and no glasses. They disappeared.

In July of 2013 the boys and I left for Dallas to spend the rest of the summer at our house there before heading to Hawaii in August. Well, when we came back I noticed our dinner glasses were gone. There was only one goblet left. They were gorgeous glass goblets. I figured I needed to teach my kids how to handle the finer things in life. I thought the best way to teach table manners and etiquette was to start when they are young. So, I have glass dishes and glass stemware that we use for every day meals. Some people may think that is weird, and that we are putting on heirs. Hey relax! The glasses cost me $1.00 each at the Dollar Tree store, and the glass dishes came in a box from Wal-Mart. A set of four costs $25.00.

Another reason I like glass has to do with my husband's fixation with drinking, or not drinking from straws. He claims the plastic is toxic. So, if the plastic from straws is toxic, what about the plastic cups and plates we have our kids drink from and eat off of, especially when they are put in the microwave? It makes sense to me, and why should I argue with my husband? I pick my battles, so we just use glass dishes and glass stemware as often as we can. We do still own plastic dishes for outside dinning, or should I say we did have plastic dishes. Now I can understand how the glass can disappear, maybe it broke and nobody is offering up any confessions. I too have been known to break a glass or two. I just figured the kids failed to tell me that they broke a glass, or several. We started out with over a dozen, and now there is only one left.

Now back to Hawaii, the reason I mentioned our trip is because the kids and I were gone for about a month. We do not lock the doors, after all we have great a great security system here on The Bigfoot Ranch in Texas. (Only a fool would dare to venture onto this property.) Well, my first assumption was that Dad broke the glasses while we were gone. No, he would probably avoid using dishes so he would not have to wash them. Then I started to wonder if while we were gone, someone else came into the house and stole the glasses. The kids used to leave them filled with milk on the coffee table, which sits directly in front of the huge patio doors and windows that line one wall in the living room. These windows face the woods. So, anything out there can see right into the living room. And what would a Juvy and Baby Squatch see? They would see glasses filled with ice cold milk. My boys always drank from these glasses and set them on the coffee table as they played on the Wii or watched TV in the living room.

Then as I was sitting there at the dinner table finishing my Christmas dinner I had started to silently inventory my dishes in my head. I started to realize that my glass square dishes were also missing. I had a set of eight, and now there were only two left. Yes, I remember breaking a few in the microwave, but six? Then I wondered what happened to all the pink plastic cereal bowls, they were all gone too, and you cannot break those. The pink 16 oz. plastic cups that cannot break either. Then I think loudly in my head, "WE HAVE LIVED HERE EXACTLY TWO YEARS!" "WHERE ALL MY DISHES?"

Okay, I know sometimes the kids feed the dogs leftovers, and I make a huge fuss if they leave my glass dishes outside, so they know to bring them in right away. We have even gone over this, "put the food in their dog bowls and bring the dishes back inside." Over and over again we tell them. Then I started obsessing over this small white *Corning Ware* bowl that I have only used once, a gift from my husband and the kids. It came with a set, very nice, microwaveable and dishwasher safe, it does not break, that is what the box said, unbreakable. Where is my perfect little dish that I only got to use once? I started thinking about how perfect that would be for my perfect mashed potatoes. Then I asked my son where the bowl was, since I remembered he was the one who was asked to take the leftovers to the dogs when I made homemade potato soup a few weeks ago. He looked at me and shrugged his shoulders. (You know, some more of that nonverbal communication I was talking about before. And you don't believe in telepathy! Please!) Then he ran outside and looked around the yard and found nothing, no plastic bowls, no cups, no glass dishes, absolutely nothing.

Then the fog slowly started to lift and I asked my husband if he had thrown away the dishes that could have possibly been accidentally left outside by us. He looked at me with a stone cold serious face and said "no," and then followed it with that look. That look is new. Remember he did not have that look the first year. He had that look now. He had that look on his face that basically said, "You know who it is." I turn around and walk to the kitchen feeling like such an idiot. I had not realized for two years that my dishes were disappearing, or being stolen, or borrowed. I do not know. This all happened right under my nose. I felt so stupid not to have noticed sooner.

Then I started to think that all the other tenants never got to this point. They just moved out within six months and figured they lost or left dishes behind. I was actually sitting there taking an inventory of all of my dishes.

Do you realize how many dishes were missing? I was now trying to remember if I had a glass goblet outside during the summer while the kids were playing in the pool, and I am almost sure I did. I love iced tea in a glass in the summer. So, I probably left one outside and it disappeared. Thinking the kids or my husband had brought it in; I got another one the next day. I know a few broke in the dishwasher, but the whole set is gone. I know I started with more than twelve. Then there are the plastic dishes that did not break and cannot break. They must have been left outside, and now they have all disappeared.

I am not mad or upset. I just cannot believe I never noticed. I am really not surprised either. We normally do not leave things outside. We do not want to give them a reason to lurk around the house at night, but they do anyway. The only things that do get left outside on occasion are the dishes, and they seemed to have disappeared.

I cleared the table and washed the dishes, the ones I had left, and decided to quickly write all of this down. I immediately grabbed a notebook and a pen and began to write this all down. I doubt I will forget it, but things seem to be happening at a much faster pace, or I am becoming much more aware this time, and much faster, and I cannot seem to keep up with all the activity.

It all makes perfect sense. It is so obvious what our dishes are used for, they are utensils. They are basic tools that we use to eat and drink. These are life sustaining activities. Can you imagine how valuable these utensils are to them? I am not trying to think like a Squatch, I am just using common sense. I mean a bowl is important to a dog or a cat. They know where their food and water bowls are and they know what comes in them. Just ask any pet lover, their pets even have their favorite bowls. It is so basic it does not even need explaining or further analysis. Dishes are extremely important to us human beings. We give them as graduation gifts and wedding gifts. It is symbolic. You are giving someone a gift as they venture out into the world to start a new life of their own. We do not have to travel very far back into history to discover how important it was to have pots to cook in or water tight containers in which to carry water. We can look at our own human history and the various cultures, goblets, glasses, pottery, porcelain, all have a place in history. Visit a museum and see how important these utensils were to "uncivilized" as well as "civilized" people, from nobility to servants dishes were very important. Now imagine how valuable these dishes are to the people in the woods.

As I am writing this I go back to the orange I received as a gift. Of course they know how to cut. Of course they have knives! They have real nice glass goblets too!! Once again I look up to the heavens with an audible sigh and a huge roll of the eyes and loudly proclaim, "Really?" "Really?" "You expect me to believe all of this?" "Do you expect anyone to believe any of this?" "I mean after all I am sitting right here in my kitchen and I don't believe any of this!"

So now I don't feel so guilty after all. Apparently even though I thought I hadn't "given" a "gift" in return to that adorable little creature who gave my adorable little sons a soccer ball and a basketball two years ago. I have come to realize that without my knowledge, we have been gifting back and forth the whole damn time! That was a mighty expensive crusty old soccer ball. It was the gift that kept on giving. Ha, ha ha! Unbelievable!

Susan Sullivan

Chapter Fifteen
The Beginning Of A New Year

The year wasn't over yet. We had more activity before the year was over. We had a water pipe break on the side of the house. I knew immediately who it was, since we were notified by someone jumping on the roof. When we didn't jump up and tend to the broken pipe, they once again tried to alert us by creating such a loud noise that can only be described as a thousand pound creature throwing themselves up against the front of the house near the front door. I was standing right next to the door in the foyer. I heard the door crack. Every evening when the sun is going down, I can see all the cracks in the door. The sun has to hit it just right and you can see sunlight beaming through all the cracks.

Recently we had another pipe break again. This time the property manager had each water faucet outside encased in cement. This time she understood what was going on. I had a book signing at the local library. I knew she would be there, don't ask me how, I just knew. I was prepared with my speech, I had even practiced what I would say when she showed up. When she walked in, and realized I was Susan Sullivan, she smiled and took a look at the book. I then turned to the page in the first book that describes the lovely property manager. She claimed I had embellished since she didn't recognize herself. We chuckled and then I told her "my" truth. She then took one look at me and leaned in and said, "Is that why everybody left?" I almost had the wind knocked right out of me. "What do you think?" "Well", she said. "I have always wondered, but nobody ever said anything, they just left." She wanted me to make one correction in the book. All of the previous tenants did receive their deposits back. What a noble woman!

What a year it has been, one we will never forget. The year ended as it had begun, with a bang. The bang of a metal pipe breaking, and the loud bang up against the front of the house. We spent the first day of the New Year repairing the broken water pipe and waiting for whatever was to come next. Little did I know that once again, within twenty four hours my world would be turned upside down. My view and opinion of the Bigfoot/Sasquatches would completely change, it would take me to the deepest darkest parts of my soul and cause me to take a step back and truly analyze what I think they are, who they are, and where they come from. It would also cause me to question who we are, and where we come from and what our connections are to the Sasquatch people.

On Jan the 2nd of 2014, exactly two years to the day that we heard the first loud thousand pound creature on the roof, the most life altering terrifying experience happened to us. Yes, it involved the Sasquatches. All of them.

Conclusion

As I sit here in my sitting room writing the first five chapters, it is freezing outside. The temperature is in the twenties tonight and I am assuming they are huddled somewhere in their camp or homestead. I begin to wonder if they know how to use fire, they seem to be intrigued by ours. I take a break and begin to play a game of solitaire. It is between 11:00 p.m. and 12:00 midnight. I am sitting here engrossed in a game when I realize I had been hearing several bumps and thumps against the side of the house, just on the other side of my desk and computer screen. I just continued to ignore the noise as I try to unwind. Then the sound is more consistent. Then I begin to look over my shoulder and wonder if someone is looking through the windows watching me play solitaire. Then I hear it again, something being thrown at the roof. All the animals (dogs and cats) are inside due to the deep freeze. I jump up and run to the living room and my boys are sound asleep on the couch and my husband is folding laundry. Then I realize it is just another night on the Bigfoot Ranch here in the woods of central Texas. They are just reminding me that they are still here.

Is this my life? Is this what my life is all about now? Am I supposed to continue this dialogue between you and me? I have come to the conclusion that my mission in life is to educate people about Bigfoot/Sasquatch. I have a funny feeling I have succeeded.

Now you find me at the end of my book. It is August 2014. It is over 100 degrees outside. I keep asking myself why this is taking so long to get finished. Then I realize with the constant disruptions, I am surprised I can write at all. Just yesterday the dogs went crazy for the second night in a row. Something was outside. The day before, we realized it was because Zack had left the water on again. They don't like that. They really are consistent. They don't like us to waste water. Last night we couldn't understand what all the commotion was about. Then today, as I am editing one last time, and adding the finishing touches and closing the book on this last section of the book, I hear it in the distance. Then the sound becomes louder and clearer, and then I realize there are hunters in the nearby woods. Once again, I am ending with a bang! Just as I had begun the second year. How very perfect and how very telling of what our life is like on The Bigfoot Ranch in Texas.

Notes From The Author

Before I go there are a few things I would like to address. I spent many months researching various aspects of the Bigfoot phenomena. I chose not to include this research in my book. I didn't want to just throw it out either. I learned so much and came to some serious conclusions based on my research. So, if you are still interested in my ramblings and my thought process, then please read on. Many of these added thoughts are based not only on my own search for understanding, but also many questions that were emailed to me by many readers and followers and people who are desperately in search of the truth.

Juvy In A Tree

The first year was really difficult for me to draw what Daphene and I had seen jump out of the tree down the driveway. When I felt more relaxed, I took the opportunity to sit down and calmly draw what we had both seen. I am not an artist, but this is basically what the creature looked like the night we spotted him. He was tall and skinny. He was covered in black hair. We never saw his face. He jumped out of a tree off of a limb that was at least 15 feet in the air. He took off and ran so fast, he disappeared as soon as he hit the ground.

First, The Body.

Okay, I heard all that talk of some guy coming down to Texas and killing a Bigfoot. The second I heard it I knew he was a liar and a fake. I just want to set the record straight. First of all, the guy was not a Texan. He was from Georgia, and he was not a hunter. I am insulted as a Texan that the public could possibly believe that some "Bigfoot Hunter" from somewhere else could come down to Texas for a weekend, visit a homeless campground, and shoot three Bigfoot/Sasquatches on the spot. Hunters know that just doesn't happen. No one is that lucky, and I don't mean lucky that he shot one, but lucky to have even had the opportunity to see one. Most people are trying to find these creatures out in the woods, and spend twenty years researching, and never even get one sighting. The very leader of the Bigfoot community, Jeff Meldrum reported in an interview that the closest he has come to a sighting is through night vision equipment that had a heat signature on it. So not even the esteemed Dr. Jeff has actually seen a Bigfoot. Also, Cliff Barackman, gave an interview this spring and also admitted to never having seen a Bigfoot. Yet this guy comes down to Texas, meets three, gets a video, and they stand there long enough so he can get a shot off, and manages to kill at least two?

I had so many people ask me what I thought. My first reaction was shock. I was shocked that people believed the lie. I live here on the ranch, maybe 2 to 3 hours away from San Antonio., and the Bigfoot/Sasquatches don't come right up to us out in the open. They hide in the trees. Also, they are not reddish brown here, they are black. I have been so startled when I am walking by a window and see a dark shadow standing at the base of a tree. I always have to take a second look. The trees are so overgrown you can't really see them, you just see the dark shadow. The only reason I can honestly say that it is a Bigfoot is because I know what the tree normally looks like. I know when they are standing under the tree because the base of the tree is dark black. I have to chuckle sometimes because I get that they are trying so hard to camouflage themselves by standing perfectly still. Yet, I can see them! There have been times that I bust out laughing because I can see the dark images of the bottom half, while the upper half is obscured by foliage. It is exactly like playing hide and seek with a three year old, who thinks you can't see them because they have placed a blanket over their head. Yet, you still see them.

One day during the first year there was this tree way across the ranch, about a half mile or more away from the house. It was bare, no leaves, probably dead, but stood taller amongst the rest because it was sitting on higher ground on the other side of the ranch. I could see it. It was white, since the bark had fallen off. It was also during the fall since all the other trees were also bare. I remember the day I noticed something unusual. Out of the blue one day the tree had a section that was black. I stared at it for the longest time. I kept walking by the window and I would just stare because the thing would not move. I am so sure it was convinced that it was camouflaged, except for the fact that this tree trunk was white. This thing stayed up there for three days and didn't move an inch. I am guessing that the ones who "allow" themselves to be seen, are the younger ones. They haven't learned their stealth skills yet. I have seen the outline or image of the bigger ones, but I can't be sure. I understand they blend in really well.

So, when I read, and saw the fake video of the Sasquatch at the homeless camp coming out into the open during daylight and allowing itself to be filmed and then shot, I knew it was all a fake. So, if you are interested in my opinion, regard all videos with skepticism. They don't like to be photographed. I believe the ones that "allow" themselves to be filmed are the younger ones, they haven't honed their skills yet, and they don't know any better. The older ones have "other" abilities that keeps them camouflaged. That is all I will say for now, I plan to write more about that in my upcoming Short Stories Books.

I had lunch with a researcher who mentioned his fear that someone was going to shoot one someday. I asked him if he wanted me to relieve his fear. I told him, they can't be captured and they can't be shot. Trust me. Yes, originally in the 1700 to 1800's there were reports of Bigfoots being shot. I believe that is because they had no knowledge of our weapons or their capabilities. Yes, Patty allowed herself to be filmed, that era also marked the birth and the beginning of the portable video camera age. She didn't know any better either. Have we seen another Patty? No, someone sent the memo out and alerted the rest. Yes, I do believe some get shot at, like the one I mentioned in an earlier chapter, and some get caught on film, but I do believe those are the younger ones, who still have much to learn. They range from six, seven to eight feet tall. The older, more mature Squatches begin at ten feet.

Which brings me to the yahoo in the Sierras that claims he shot a mama and a baby. I saw that video reenactment on Monsters and Mysteries in America. Okay before I could sit and analyze the story and the outlandish claims, just let me describe to you how I reacted when I saw this story. I am a normal human being. Okay, not really, I am a little more sensitive than most. I did not know what was going to happen. I was glued to the television set. I thought, "Why would he shoot at them from the truck, he wasn't in any danger?" Then he pulled the trigger. I jumped up and felt the wind leave my chest and my knees buckled. Then he shot the baby. I screamed as if my own child had been shot. My family came running to my room and I couldn't even get the words out, I cried and cried. Just writing this my eyes are filling with tears, even though I know the guy is a psychopath and a liar. I cried in a way that I have never heard myself cry. It actually frightened me. It came from someplace so deep within my soul. I hated that man. I felt a rage and anger from within me, and I wanted him dead. That is really unusual for me since I am rather passive. It took me a few days to gather my thoughts. I cannot watch the shooting again. What I can watch is the interview. When I looked into the shooter's eyes, I saw into the eyes of a psychopath who is totally detached from reality. I knew he was a liar. Or, he has such a low IQ that he doesn't have a conscience and his actions don't register, also like the individual I described earlier. Notice how he doesn't blink during the whole interview. He doesn't sweat and his heart rate never changes. There is no reaction. Now, there was another man on a Bigfoot program. I watched him as he was interviewed about a five second sighting that occurred twenty years ago. His eyes were shifting, he was blinking, and sweating and you can see the blood vessel in his neck pumping, it was actually bulging from the blood rushing to his head. That my friend is what someone who has had a Bigfoot encounter looks like. I start stuttering when I talk about my sightings. The words and thoughts start coming out so fast that I make absolutely no sense when I am speaking. That is why it helps me to write it all down. So look upon all videos, pictures, and evidence with skepticism, and make note of people's physiological responses. Learn to be a human lie detector. We all react the same to stress. We all have physiological responses to fear. If there is absolutely no response, there may be other factors to consider, psychopathological tendencies or a total lack of knowledge or intelligence. It is hard to detect that in writing, so I will just say this, I am open to meeting people. I have met several people who have come to Texas and asked to sit and meet me. These meetings are long and in depth and allows you to see my experiences through my eyes and in my words. Even after two years, and two books, I react with panic in my voice. My heart races and I begin to stutter. I can't seem to get the words out fast enough. Then there is a point where I reach maximum overload and I start to shut down, I can't even put a sentence together to describe what has happened. Yes, there is an actual point where I am at a loss for words. My husband will tell you that this is a rare moment!

Science

Ah the DNA. Yes, we have all heard about the DNA. First we heard about the Ketchum study. I still don't know what to think about that one since there is not enough information on the subject to allow me to form an honest opinion. Believe it or not folks, you are allowed to suspend your opinion until further information is presented to allow you to make an informed opinion. I can't stand it when people just throw their opinion around without serious thought and proper analysis. Yes, I realize everyone has an opinion, but everyone shouldn't be giving one. I am smart enough to know how to suspend mine. So, that is what I think about the Ketchum DNA study.

Now the new study that came out of the U.K. I know a little about that. I had seen the documentary and was stunned that they were quantifying that as "scientific" evidence. One of the samples was given by the individual I spoke of earlier who claimed to have shot a Mama and Baby Sasquatch in the Sierras. At the moment I realized he was part of the study, I knew the results would be invalid. I was shocked by the method of collection. Remember the Sierra guy, he went back a year later to collect DNA. Really? Then another fellow on the show went into the woods and saw hair and "assumed" they were Bigfoot hair. The sample was in no way connected to a sighting, sounds, or tracks, he just happened to see the hair and decided to collect it. Now I had a Bigfoot in my backyard. I saw the Juvy in the Backyard near the pool. I could place both the Juvy and hair in the same place at the same time and yet I did not collect the DNA from the pool filter. I honestly believed, that unless I could actually without question know that the hair came from a Bigfoot body, there was no need to collect the sample. So I was stunned by the method of collection used in the documentary. Not at all following scientific protocol. There are methods and standards for collection and not one of them was used. So of course the study would prove that most of the DNA samplings were of known species.

Unfortunately, the only way we will get an honest DNA sample is if a Bigfoot shows up at a blood drive. Other than that, we aren't getting one. I can live with that. I don't need a DNA sample. Besides our awareness of DNA and genetics is fairly new. What did we do before DNA was recognized and discovered? Aah. We relied on eyewitness testimony! Go figure!!! I also don't think we should hold our breath and wait for a body to show up. I don't think it will ever happen. I have heard from several sources that a body has already been collected, these creatures have already been studied, and apparently the powers that be did not like the answers. I read it all over the internet, the claims that they were studied at UC Berkeley. I researched employees, professors, and timelines. I tried to make the connections. Then I read an article that claimed that Stephen Hawking was involved in the study. Someone in the article asked, "Why hasn't anyone asked him, instead of all this speculating?" So, I did just that. I found his email, wrote him a letter and asked if he would be willing to talk to me. I received a response from his assistant and was told he was unavailable for such requests. Oh well, I tried.

I believe if we were told the truth about Bigfoot, and his origins, we wouldn't like the answers either. So, I believe we are purposefully being kept in the dark. That is why I believe the government doesn't get involved and remains silent. I was shocked that the guy pulling around a fake Bigfoot and charging hardworking people $20, would have been of interest to the IRS, but they didn't seem to care either. Then I wondered if letting him prop up this fake, and allowing this fraud to play out to the end would only serve to benefit those who want to keep the truth about Bigfoot a secret. And, that is exactly what happened. People started saying, if that is a fake, then they are all fakes. That is okay with me. The more people think it is a fake, the less likely they are to go out into the woods and hunt and stalk them. And the less likely they are to show up at my place.

Paranoramal Bigfoot? What?

I intentionally left out so much research for fear that people would not be interested. I realized all the research I had done was based on my new awareness. I had not known of the paranormal aspects of Bigfoot until the beginning of the 3rd year. The second year was all about the ongoing process of discovering who they were. I too thought they were just flesh and blood creatures. It was as if they patiently allowed me to take the time I needed to become aware of what I was dealing with. They were no longer trying to scare me out of the house and off the property. They too were trying to discover who I was. So much of the research would not have made sense since I would have been way ahead of the story. I plan to slowly introduce new stories with some of this research to compliment the new paranormal experiences we continue to have during the 3rd year. What I will do is leave you with this. I know now why so many people thought the house was haunted. It all makes perfect sense now. They weren't crazy, and I believe every word they told me. I absolutely believe they experienced everything they described, which I now know is the paranormal side of the Bigfoot Phenomena.

Bibliography

http://www.tpwd.state.tx.us/huntwild/wild/nuisance/feral_hogs/

http://feralhogs.tamu.edu/about/

http://ww2.txhoghunting.com/app/news/24744/Business-is-hog-wild-for-Milam-County-trapper

http://news.harvard.edu/gazette/story/2008/04/eating-meat-led-to-smaller-stomachs-bigger-brains/

http://www.washingtonpost.com/national/health-science/sorry-vegans-eating-meat-and-cooking-food-is-how-humans-got-their-big-brains/2012/11/26/3d4d36de-326d-11e2-bb9b-288a310849ee_story.html

http://www.berkeley.edu/news/media/releases/99legacy/6-14-1999a.html

http://www.sunstar-solutions.com/BFgeological.htm

http://www.bigfootencounters.com/biology/migration.htm

www.innerspacecavern.com

www.longhorncaverns.com

www.naturalbridgecaverns.com

www.texasbigfootinmybackyard.com